T0361236

FOREIGN AID AND ECONOMIC GROWTH

Foreign Aid and Economic Growth

A theoretical and empirical investigation

JANINE L. BOWEN
Department of Economics and Management
Goucher College
Baltimore, Maryland

Routledge
Taylor & Francis Group

LONDON AND NEW YORK

First published 1998 by Ashgate Publishing

Reissued 2018 by Routledge
2 Park Square, Milton Park, Abingdon, Oxon, OX14 4RN
52 Vanderbilt Avenue, New York, NY 10017

Routledge is an imprint of the Taylor & Francis Group, an informa business

Copyright © Janine L. Bowen 1998

All rights reserved. No part of this book may be reprinted or reproduced or utilised in any form or by any electronic, mechanical, or other means, now known or hereafter invented, including photocopying and recording, or in any information storage or retrieval system, without permission in writing from the publishers.

Notice:
Product or corporate names may be trademarks or registered trademarks, and are used only for identification and explanation without intent to infringe.

Publisher's Note
The publisher has gone to great lengths to ensure the quality of this reprint but points out that some imperfections in the original copies may be apparent.

Disclaimer
The publisher has made every effort to trace copyright holders and welcomes correspondence from those they have been unable to contact.

A Library of Congress record exists under LC control number:

ISBN 13: 978-0-367-07500-2 (hbk)
ISBN 13: 978-0-429-02104-6 (ebk)

Contents

Tables and figures

Preface and acknowledgments

A great deal has been written about foreign aid and economic development. Academic libraries are filled with books dealing with a wide variety of interrelated issues and debates about the development process and the role of foreign capital. Perhaps the most common element in these books is their discussion of the many reasons foreign aid does not (and perhaps cannot) achieve all or any of its many objectives, of which economic growth in recipient countries is only one.

This book does provide an overview of the fundamental issues surrounding foreign aid effectiveness, yet its primary objective is narrow. While recognizing the legitimacy and importance of examining obstructions to aid effectiveness (whether they be from the donor, the recipient, or the complex system of external concessional finance), the question remains if and how foreign aid has affected economic growth in recipient countries. It is somewhat surprising that given the volumes of writing about why aid can or cannot improve economic growth or speed the development 'process' (in a particular country or in general), little work has been put forth to assess the actual impact of aid on economic growth in recipient countries over time. Thus the primary focus of this work is to investigate the effect years of foreign aid have had on economic growth rates, despite the many problems and complications that may hinder maximum effectiveness.

I am deeply indebted to Dr. Emilio Casetti who introduced me to the expansion methodology as an approach to answering my research questions, and who provided invaluable assistance and guidance throughout this study. I would also like to thank Dr. Stephen Mangum and Dr. Sven Lundstedt for their careful reading of, and incisive comments on, an earlier version of this study. Finally I would like to acknowledge the support of Goucher College during the writing of this book.

1 Introduction

The purpose of this book is to assess what effect official development assistance (ODA) has had on economic growth rates in sixty-seven recipient countries over a nineteen year period. It is important to first understand the historical context in which aid flows exist. How did this complex system of concessional financing between nation-states begin? The best marker to denote the beginnings of this system is the creation of the World Bank and the US Marshall Plan just following World War II. Bilateral aid agencies, regional development banks, and coordinating groups soon followed. Their actions can be understood in large part in the context of the Cold War, with recipient countries as squares on a global chess board and the US and Soviet Union as the key players. But there were other motivations as well, some more or less altruistic. Today the Cold War is over and Japan, rather than the US, is the largest donor nation. But the aid flows under examination here should be considered within the historical context that created them.

Allotments of concessional financing and assistance were of course not to be used at the discretion of recipients but rather were designed and implemented by donors. In the 1960's donors focused largely on capital-intensive, state-building projects. In the 1970's programs to meet basic human needs in recipient countries were emphasized. By the 1980's and the international debt crisis, non-project based or rather program-based lending became more common to more directly influence the public policies and economic structures of recipient states. This trend has continued in the 1990's. Today, well over one-hundred countries receive a total of more than $50 billion annually from donors, whose numbers have also continued to increase.

There is no shortage of discussion regarding the motives and objectives behind donor actions (and those of recipients, for that matter). There is also no shortage of debate as to whether, and to what extent, the system has been beneficial or detrimental to recipient countries. What does seem to be lacking, however, is sufficient empirical evidence on which to base these discussions and debates. Of course the number of questions in need of empirical investigation can be overwhelming. Only one is investigated here: what effect has aid had on economic growth rates in sixty-seven recipient countries over a nineteen year period? The answer, it is hoped, will better inform the important discussions and debates about the past and the possibilities for the future.

Just as evidence from empirical studies should inform discussion and debate, empirical studies should be informed by theoretical understandings of the relationships under examination. Thus a number of theoretical schools of thought about the relationship between foreign capital and economic growth are reviewed here to provide the first step in constructing an empirical study of aid effectiveness. In short, liberal economic theory foresees a positive impact from foreign capital on economic growth; theorists from the dependency school and its offshoots foresee a negative impact; and contemporary mercantilists foresee that the role of the recipient nation-state is the primary determinant of the impact of foreign capital.

Any empirical study should also be informed by its predecessors. Here, 34 previous studies of the role of foreign capital (and aid more specifically) in economic growth are reviewed. The most striking features of this review are lack of dialogue between researchers across theoretical perspectives and lack of consistency in their findings even within theoretical perspectives. The strength and nature of the aid-growth relationship remains unclear after more than forty years of foreign aid programs, nearly a trillion dollars in aid disbursements, and numerous studies of the impact aid has had on economic growth in recipient countries. Results vary from significantly positive (Papanek 1973; Over 1975; Stoneman 1975; Dowling and Hiemenz 1983; Mosley, Hudson, and Horrell 1992), to significantly negative (Griffin and Enos 1970; Mosley, Hudson and Horrell 1987), to nonsignificant (Mosley 1980, 1987; Rana and Dowling 1988; Landau 1990).

Typically, studies of aid effectiveness have used multiple regression to relate economic growth (the dependent variable) to variables, imported from theory and from previous empirical research, which are widely believed to contribute to economic growth. Aid was then added to the list of independent variables. The effectiveness of aid in contributing to economic growth was proved or disproved by the significance and sign of the aid coefficient, as well as by the amount of explained variance in economic growth.

This study contends that results from previous studies have in aggregate been inconclusive largely because of methodological limitations and that a significant aid-growth relationship does exist.   Further, the nature of the relationship (for example, positive or negative) varies across levels of economic development.

2

More specifically, this study proposes to test if and how the traditional model of economic growth varies across levels of economic aid to determine more exactly how aid may act as a modifier of other relationships between growth and its determinants. The methodology to be employed is the expansion methodology (Casetti 1972, 1986, 1990), which allows an initial model to be expanded into a model that is more responsive to its environment or context. That is to say, from expansion methodology, an initial model of economic growth in less-developed countries can become a model that better explains the aid-growth relationship by incorporating the relationships aid may have with other determinants of economic growth.

Following discussion of the historical context for aid programs (Chapter 2), a review of theoretical perspectives on foreign capital in recipient countries (Chapter 3), and a review of previous studies of aid effectiveness (Chapter 4), the methodological approach of this study is introduced (Chapter 5). Chapter 6 provides results of tests on the traditional model of economic growth and indication of their robustness. Further investigation and explanation of the results, including testing of an alternative model of economic growth, follow to provide additional insight into the key relationship between aid and growth. Finally, a discussion of the study and additional comments on the relevance of this study to the future effectiveness of the international aid regime are provided.

2   Historical Context

Evolution of the regime

Foreign aid has historical roots that extend back to the nineteenth century. In fact, transferring money on concessional terms to the governments of colonies was common practice by the turn of the century. Britain, France, Germany and the United States all transferred funds under the label 'infant colony subsidies' before 1914 (Mosley, 1987). French aid to the United States played a crucial role in the Revolutionary War against Great Britain, and US military aid to allied states helped counterbalance Nazi Germany during World War II.

The phenomenon of foreign economic aid as it is understood today, however, originates from the aftermath of the second World War. In 1944, delegates from 40 countries agreed in Bretton Woods, New Hampshire, to create institutions for a new monetary system and a multilateral world economy. Among the newly created institutions was the World Bank, which came into existence in December of 1945. Its primary objective was to make financial resources available to war-torn economies of Europe. It became the basis for multilateral aid. Also at this time, a number of colonized nations gained their independence and became candidates for foreign aid. In 1946, however, the United States shifted its European development funds back to bilateral mechanisms by creating the European Recovery Program (leaving the Bank with only a minor role during the years of European reconstruction). After the creation of the bilateral US program and a UN program for European reconstruction, the Bank shifted its focus toward development in the poorer countries.

The European Recovery Program, better known as the Marshall Plan (named after General George C. Marshall), provided $497 million in reconstruction loans in 1947 and disbursed more than $13 billion dollars by 1952, 89 percent of which went to Europe (Brown, 1953). Other recipients included non-

4

European states such as Korea, the Philippines, Taiwan and Turkey. By all accounts the Plan was a great success, and was largely credited for the rapid economic growth rates of Western European economies by the early 1950's.

As the Marshall Plan ended, the 1953 Mutual Security Act established a new US foreign aid program, though the US commitment to assisting less developed countries came earlier in the 'Fourth Point' of President Harry S. Truman's 1949 inaugural speech:

> Fourth, we must embark on a bold new program for making the benefits of our scientific advance and technical progress available for the improvement and growth of under-developed areas...I believe we should make available to peace-loving peoples the benefits of our store of technical knowledge in order to help them realize their aspirations for a better life. And in cooperation with other nations, we should foster capital investment in areas needing development...(from Browne, p. 14).

> Among its primary objectives, the Truman administration attempted to establish a postwar political and economic order that would encourage (and reward) democratic governments that pursued liberal macroeconomic policies. Secondary objectives included reestablishing markets for exports from the United States and Western Europe, helping domestic manufacturers and farmers dispose of surplus stocks, bolstering allies who had liquidated their overseas investments during the war and faced the impending loss of colonial possessions, and preserving the good-will of LDC's as sources of raw materials and potential markets needed by the United States and other industrialized states (Hook, 1995, p. 24).

From the onset, however, there was a rivalry between the US and the Soviet Union for strategic and political alignments. Aid money was often used as a tool in their struggle for dominance. Foreign aid programs in both countries were part of a broader foreign policy. "Following on the heels of US military victory in World War II, the success of the Marshall Plan contributed mightily to the belief that the limits of US foreign policy were on a distant and receding horizon" (Wood, 1986). Although its modelers envisioned the need for foreign aid to be temporary, the Marshall Plan served as a precursor for permanent concessional external financing within the postwar world.

Other countries began 'donating' aid funds during the 1950's. Key recipients included newly independent India and other countries in southern Asia. The Soviet Union's Council for Mutual Economic Assistance (CMEA) established additional aid programs.

A number of important developments occurred during the early 1960's, particularly in 1960. First, the International Development Association (IDA) was created as a concessional lending facility within the World Bank. Its primary objective was to lend long-term, interest-free loans to the poorer developing countries. Also during 1960, the Development Assistance Group was created from within the Organization for European Economic Cooperation (OEEC), which was later reconstituted as the Organization for Economic Cooperation and Development (OECD). The Assistance Group was renamed the Development Assistance Committee (DAC) in 1961. The DAC became "the leading forum of the richer nations for discussing their mutual interests involved in the policies, administration and effectiveness of aid" (Rubin, 1966, p. 4). In addition to its practical significance, the DAC was symbolic in bringing together the Marshall Plan aid partners and Japan. It included a research center and provided monitoring of aid trends. The DAC has played a key role in determining Western responses to development needs (Browne, 1990). Finally, within the same year, 16 countries (primarily in West Africa) gained independence. And the developing countries became a formidable group within the United Nations, comprising two-thirds of the membership.

The following year aid administration agencies were formed in main donor countries, including the US Agency for International Development (USAID), the ministries for Cooperation in France and West Germany, and the Overseas Economic Cooperation Fund in Japan. The US targeted Latin America while other donors targeted Asia and Africa. (Since then, virtually every developed country has established a foreign assistance program, with great variability in their objectives). Also in 1961, the United Nations declared the decade to be the first 'Development Decade'. Targets for resource transfers (including aid and private investment) from developed to developing countries were set at one percent of the combined donor country incomes (the target was changed to 0.7 percent of GNP for the second 'Development Decade'). Optimism seemed to be in the air for the possibilities of development and self-sustaining growth in the third world.

By the mid 1960's, three regional development banks had also formed: the Inter-American Development Bank (IDB) in 1959, the African Development Bank (AfDB) in 1964, and the Asian Development Bank (ADB) in 1966. And by the end of the decade, consensus had been reached for a formal definition of aid, termed 'official development assistance', to distinguish it from other resource flows.

Throughout the 1960's, donors were focused largely on decolonization and state-building across the Third World. Aid flows doubled, and "the institutional basis of the contemporary aid regime was established" (Hook, p. 25). Despite the influence of developing countries to attract attention to their plight, and the optimism of aid proponents everywhere, the intended beneficiaries (disadvantaged peoples of the developing world) remained victims.

Their representatives, encouraged to believe that aid would contribute crucially to development progress, had placed it high on the world agenda. But aid flows would continue to be subject mainly to the wills of the largest donors whose responses, except in the case of short-term relief campaigns, were tied more to immediate domestic economic exigencies than to broader development needs (Browne, p. 24).

Within and beyond the flurry of activity in the aid 'business', critical questions and concerns began to arise as to the effect popular capital-intensive projects were having on income distribution and basic needs in developing countries. At the end of the decade, the Pearson Commission reported on the 'crisis in aid.' Focus began to shift to the causes of perpetually uneven exchanges between the developed and less developed countries. Foreign exchange earnings were being siphoned off to service mounting debt burdens. Foreign exchange earnings were already constrained by worsening terms of trade between primary and secondary products.

Donors themselves found recipients not 'repaying' them for their 'assistance' with higher demand for donor exports (as had been the case in Western Europe). Their response was to increasingly tie aid to the procurement of goods and services in the donor countries. Radicals from the left and the right began criticizing programs vehemently.

The focus on state building as a primary objective of ODA in the 1960's shifted to the promotion of 'basic human needs' in the 1970's. Concessional flows increased sevenfold during this time (Hook, p. 23). In 1973 the oil crisis from the Middle East and the food crisis in Africa led the developed countries into economic recession and many African countries into famine. At the end of the year, the second 'Development Decade' had been declared a failure and was followed by a UN program to establish a 'new international economic order'. It called for:

a new way of ordering the international economic system so as to bring about, first, improved terms of trade between the present-day center and periphery countries...; secondly, more control by the periphery over the world economic cycles that pass through them...; and, thirdly, increased and improved trade between the periphery countries themselves (Galtung, 1991, p. 287).

Reforms were recommended for international trade, development finance, foreign investment, technology transfer, and natural resource exploitation (Browne, p. 29). The third 'Development Decade' was proclaimed in 1981.

But the 1980's brought a new set of concerns. The food crisis in Africa reached new proportions. Mass media brought pictures of the starving from Ethiopia and Sudan to the public. Aid became a widely discussed topic. The debt crisis also reached a new high and was well publicized. Developing countries had been simultaneously experiencing declining demand for their exports in world markets and rising interest rates from industrialized countries. In August of 1982, Mexico moved to reschedule its debt and within a year, almost as many developing countries entered into debt rescheduling negotiations as in the previous 25 years (Kruger, 1989; World Bank, 1984). By 1988, the net transfer from developing to developed countries was $43 billion, yielding a total for the 1983-88 period of $143 billion (Browne, p. 36; World Bank, 1988).

High debt and slow economic growth remained high priority concerns at the World Bank and other multilateral and bilateral agencies. But the growth rate of aid donations fell during the 1980's, as did private flows from developed to developing countries (OECD, 1985). The aid flows that were transferred in the 1980's began to take the form of non-project, or 'program', assistance. This type of aid was first developed by the Bank in 1980 as 'structural adjustment loans'. The trend of non-project assistance that spread to numerous other agencies touched off a wide debate. On one side of the issue, domestic policies have often been partly responsible for aid ineffectiveness, and the conditions and consulting that accompany this type of aid address the appropriateness of policies in the recipient countries directly. On the other hand, conditionality at its worst erodes national sovereignty and invades the recipients' internal decision making structure with foreign interest in a manner which may be exploitative and/or may perpetuate 'dependency'.

Nonetheless, policy dialogue between donors and recipients greatly expanded during the 1980's. Respect for human rights became an additional condition during this period. Aid proponents were also pleased to see aid restored to a position of relative prominence. In 1988, as in 1960, aid contributed about half of net resource flows to developing countries, having dropped to 30 percent in 1980. The share of direct investment also rebounded in the same period (Browne, 1990; OECD, 1985).

Aid flows were at last freed from Cold War politics with the fall of Communism in the early 1990's. And volumes were expected to increase from the so-called 'peace dividend'. Wealthy governments pledged higher levels of foreign aid at the 1992 UN Conference on Environment and Development to address a wide range of transnational problems. "For a fleeting moment it appeared that foreign aid, for so long contaminated by the Cold War, would finally achieve its vast potential" (Hook, 1996, p.1).

To the contrary, aid in absolute terms and as a proportion of donor GNP fell to its lowest levels in two decades (OECD, 1996a, p. 89) and living standards in recipient countries worsened. Real per capita income in fifty-one low and middle income countries was lower in 1993 than in 1980, and overall gross domestic product fell in 14 countries. Life expectancy among low income countries averaged 62 years in 1993 compared to 77 years for high income economies; infant mortality in the poorest countries averaged 64 per 1,000 live births; nine times the level recorded in affluent states (Hook, p. 2; World Bank, 1995a; World Bank, 1982). "As many newly industrialized countries (NICs) enjoyed rapid economic growth and attracted large amounts of both public and private capital, the growing income gaps shattered what little remained of a cohesive 'Third World'. This is the setting in which to explore the current status and future prospects of foreign aid" (Hook, p. 3).

The historical context of aid flows has been characterized as an evolving international aid regime. Robert Wood (1980, 1986) linked the concept of an international regime (Keohane and Nye, 1977; Krasner, 1982, 1983) with the world-system perspective to describe a foreign aid regime (Lockwood, p. 49). The regime consists of increasingly coordinated and routinized aid programs from across donor countries, that continue to meet donor interests and larger foreign policy goals more so than the needs of many recipients (Hook, 1995). From the world-system perspective, the regime ensures the recipient governments adopt policies and approaches likened to a 'golden straightjacket' (Friedman, 1997), such as private ownership, openness to trade and investment, a floating currency value, membership in supranational organizations, etc.; overall, a reduced role of the state. These features systematically limit the opportunities for state controlled development" (Lockwood, p. 50). Though Friedman's 'golden straightjacket' referred to government policies adopted in the era of globalization, his comments are equally applicable to aid recipients. "The golden straightjacket reduces national politics to a choice between Coke and Pepsi" (Friedman, 1997).

When applied to foreign aid, the regime concept means that there exists among bilateral and multilateral donors widely shared views about the conditions that should govern access to concessional external financing and about the general type of development access should encourage (Lockwood, p. 49).

As implied by the selected quotes below, recognition that aid programs exist within the context of larger foreign policy goals is not new.

The sole test of foreign aid is not something to be done, as a Government enterprise, for its own sake or for the sake of others. The United States Government is not a charitable institution, nor is it an appropriate outlet for the charitable spirit of the American people (Liska, 1960, p. 127).

[F]oreign aid is first and foremost a technique of statecraft. It is, in other words, a means by which one nation tries to get other nations to act in desired ways...Thus, foreign aid policy is foreign policy, and as such it is a subject of controversy in both the international and the domestic political arenas (Baldwin, 1966, p. 3).

9

Accusations of less than altruistic motives have also been leveled at recipient governments. They have been accused of playing up the "aid rivalry" between Cold War powers and incorporating aid into long-term fiscal planning and development strategies. In sum, "foreign assistance strengthened the sense of interdependence between North and South, the most significant aspect of contemporary global relations...[I]t represents a central facet of the contemporary world order, in which the 'low politics' of social and economic welfare have become as salient to international relations as the 'high politics' of military security (Keohane and Nye, 1989; Hook, 1995, p. 16).

Trends in aid flows

Global aid flows

Levels of global aid flows have varied considerably over the years. During the 1960's global aid volumes did not grow substantially. From the early 1970's to the mid-1980's, they doubled (primarily from the DAC and the emergence of Arab donors). During the mid-1980's, aid volumes fell from nearly all sources. Toward the end of the 1980's aid donations grew consistently but at slower rates than in earlier years, and then fell off again between 1992 ($60.9 billion) and 1994 ($59.2 billion). Absolute levels of aid rebounded again in 1994. As a share of GNP, however, in 1994 OECD countries averaged only .30 percent, the lowest rate in 21 years and far from the international standard of .70 percent (OECD, 1996a, p. 89). Ratios of ODA to GNP had remained almost constant at 0.35 percent from 1970-90. Aid from Central and Eastern Europe, and from the former Soviet Union, have almost vanished but have been replaced to some degree by emerging developing country donors.

Leading donors

In the early 1960's the United states was the primary aid donor, followed by France, the UK and Germany. Japan became a major donor by 1970, along with Canada and the Netherlands. Since then, the US, France, and the UK have all lowered their ODA/GNP ratios significantly. The ratios of Australia, Canada, Denmark, the Netherlands, Norway and Sweden have increased. Today, Japan is the largest donor in absolute terms, followed by the US, France and Germany. And the number of donors has continued to grow. Ireland, Portugal, Spain and South Korea are among the most recent.

Bilateral and multilateral proportions

Most of the aid has been bilateral (averaging between 75 and 84 percent from 1970-90). Multilateral aid had expanded significantly during the early and mid-1970's but fell off in the 1980's, particularly from the US, Japan and Italy. The share of multilateral aid to the total was about 35 percent in the early 1980's but fell to less than 30 percent by 1994. Nordic countries and Canada have continually led DAC members in terms of the share of their aid that goes to multilateral sources.

Leading recipients

In terms of distribution, a much larger proportion of aid went to Sub-Saharan Africa and to the Middle East (including Egypt) over the past two decades. Aid shares fell in South Asia (especially India) and the Mediterranean, and increased only slightly in Central America. Much of the Sub-Saharan Africa aid came from the European Community, Nordic countries, and Canada. The US supplied much of its aid to Israel and Egypt, as well as to Africa and Central America. Japan concentrated on Asia, but also increased shares to Africa. Australia and New Zealand distributed their largest shares to Oceania and the Far East. In terms of income levels, roughly 15 percent of DAC ODA goes to upper middle-income countries; half to low-income countries; and the remainder to the least-developed countries. As of 1994 the leading recipients were Egypt ($9.7 billion), China ($9.6 billion), India ($9.1 billion), and Indonesia ($7.9 billion). Other countries to receive large increases in the early 1990's were Bolivia, Ethiopia, Uganda and Vietnam. Overall, the distribution of aid is far from even across recipients.

Other financial flows

ODA accounted for more than half of total net resource flows to developing countries in 1990. But as aid flows waned in the early 1990's, private flows expanded (e.g., direct investments, commercial bank lending, and bond lending), reaching 60 percent of all capital flows from industrialized to developing countries in 1994. The lion's share of private funds to less developed countries has gone to the emerging and transitional economies of east Asia, Eastern Europe, and the former Soviet Union. Sub-Saharan Africa, however, is almost totally dependent on financial assistance with one of the highest ODA/per capita ratios in the world. And projections for this region's official finance requirement, to reach a target growth rate of zero, has continued to grow. The least developed countries also receive very little of the private financial flows.

Capital requirements

Studies that investigate and/or determine capital requirements for target growth rates in less developed countries changed significantly since the 1960's. The models used have included the savings-gap model, the trade-gap model, and the two-gap model. Recent studies have become more sophisticated, taking interest payments on external debt into account, disaggregating capital requirements by region, and distinguishing between official and private funds. Target per capita growth rates are set to zero for low-income Africa.

A review of various projections of finance requirements for the 1990's (conducted by the World Bank, the UN, the IMF and others) was provided by Lensink and Van Bergeijk (1991). They offer an important reminder of the increasing demand for economic assistance. The projected aid requirements for the 1990's for Sub-Saharan Africa, as an example, varied around $2.5 billion annually. According to Lensink and Van Bergeijk, however, the projections are optimistic. They found that approximately $12 billion of additional official funds (roughly a doubling of ODA levels) would be necessary to halt economic decline in Sub-Saharan Africa.

If a fundamental objective in the 21st century is to create a co-operative, sustainable world order, then development assistance will be a key tool. Aid, aid agencies, and the aid policy dialogue can play an important role in contributing to the solution of global problems (OECD, 1992, p. 48).

Yet serious concerns regarding the effectiveness and importance of aid (relative to other factors) persist. "Despite the political and social energy invested in it, aid has, in itself, been a relatively unimportant direct input into the development process. Both historical record, and a quick survey across the developing world at the present time, supports this generalization" (Hayden, 1987, p. 3).

Before immersing into the historical debate over the role and impact of aid in developing countries, it is important to remain cognizant of the extent to which the debate remains unresolved. It appears as critical now as ever before to investigate carefully if and how aid may be of some substantial use to its recipients. Is the factor that most constrains aid effectiveness its quantity, its quality, the domestic policies that direct its use, or its inherent nature as an arm of foreign governments and interests?

Since the 1950's our understanding of the development process has made major advances. But we can never fully understand the consequences of any assistance activity or of intervention into complex and interdependent social systems.

Our limited knowledge about how to give and use aid to contribute most effectively to development does not, however, protect us from an obligation to assess the consequences of our strategic or development assistance and to advance our capacity to understand the role of external assistance in the development process (Ruttan, 1989, p. 421).

The theoretical and empirical investigation to follow is an attempt to do just that.

3 Theoretical Background

Introduction

Economic growth and development within so-called third world countries has been a subject of debate, on theoretical and empirical grounds, since the end of World War II. The issue has been studied and critiqued through the eyes of numerous academic fields, including economics, sociology, and political science. Still no single theory or perspective has emerged with anything nearing a consensus regarding the role of foreign capital and domestic factors in the development and growth of less developed countries. Likewise, numerous empirical studies of the role of these factors in development have also failed to achieve a consensus on their relative or absolute importance. An overview of the most well-known theoretical perspectives, and the empirical studies that have attempted to test them, will be presented here to shed some light on the source(s) of their inconsistencies and a reasonable way forward.

Economic theories of development

The subject of economic growth has been, and continues to be, a controversial area within the study of economics. Since the eighteenth century, many economists have attempted to explain economic growth, including Adam Smith, Karl Marx and Joseph Schumpeter. The period following World War II brought renewed interest in the subject. A number of different theories have resulted from the work of that time. However, there is no general theory of economic growth that can prescribe policy at all stages of economic development or for all types of economic systems. The primary difference between economic theories is the varied

14

importance assigned to different factors and the proposed relationships between those factors.

Classical theory of economic growth

Economists of the eighteenth and nineteenth century, such as Smith, Ricardo, Malthus and Mill, have been categorized as classical economists. In general, classical theorists are those which pre-date the publication of Keynes' The General Theory in 1936. Long-term growth of national income and the process by which growth occurs was their primary focus. Choi (1983, p. 21) summarized the contribution of classical economists to growth theory as follows: (1) They provided a list of crucial factors that are supposed to determine the pace of the output growth in the economy. The elements include factors of production (natural resources, capital and labor), technology, and the institutional setting of economic activity; (2) They developed certain propositional relationships among the identified elements. One well-known proposition in this regard is the effect of diminishing returns resulting from the combination of capital and labor with limited natural resources; and (3) They suggest "some ranking in the growth promoting properties of the different elements, some crucial factors on which to focus" (Deane, 1978, p. 41). The most important factor was capital accumulation.

The classical period of economics ended with the so-called Keynesian Revolution that began with the publication of Keynes' The General Theory in 1936. Keynes was primarily concerned with short-term variations in income and output. Within a decade the vast majority of economists throughout the western world were converted to the Keynesian way of thinking (Blaug, 1990, p. 25). Keynes challenged several basic assumptions of classic economic theory, including that: (1) economies are stable and are predisposed to full employment levels of output; and (2) there is no reason for government intervention to promote stability or full employment. Neither the classic economists, nor Keynes, were specifically concerned with the economic development of poor countries. But the implication drawn from the Keynesian Revolution regarding market intervention became an early building block for development theories yet to come.

The Harrod-Domar growth model

The independent, yet similar, models of Roy Harrod (1939) and Evsey Domar (1946) were built upon Keynesian economics. They have been most closely identified with the establishment of a theory derived from Keynesian thought (Browne, 1990, p. 102). Like the classic economists, they assigned an important role to growth of capital formation from investment. Also like their predecessors, neither was particularly concerned with developing countries per se. Their work was the beginning of a modern growth theory that extended Keynes' focus on short-run aggregate demand to the long-term, and expressed a relationship between savings, investment and income such that an economy would grow smoothly with full employment (Domar, 1946; Harrod, 1939). The extension of Keynes' theory into the long run led to development of the incremental capital-output ratio (the amount of capital formation associated with a given increase in output).

Both economists proposed that within a country, and over time, the capital-output ratio was stable. Therefore an increase in investment would lead to economic growth. The approaches of Harrod and Domar were later lumped together as the Harrod-Domar model, in which it is assumed that the long-term economic equilibrium (where aggregate supply equals aggregate demand) occurs when the savings rate (S), or investment rate (I), is equal to the change in national income (Y_1-Y_0) times the capital-output ratio (v). Note that k indicates the value of capital required to produce one unit of output in a single period. Thus, $I = S = k(Y_1-Y_0)$. Stated differently, the growth rate at equilibrium is equal to the savings rate divided by the capital-output ratio. Their definition of equilibrium conditions for growth connected an objective of development (economic growth) with a major constraint on growth (investment) (Colman and Nixon, 1986, p. 24). The model was used to determine rates of saving or investment required for a target growth rate, given a certain capital-output ratio. The target rate for investment would depend on the capital-output ratio. A country with a higher capital-output ratio must increase the investment rate more than a country with a lower capital-output ratio, to reach the same target growth rate.

The simplified version of the Harrod-Domar model can be represented by one functional equation:

$$\Delta Y_t = 1/v \; \Delta K_t = 1/v \; I_t \tag{1}$$

and two identities,

$$I_t - S_t = M_t - X_t \tag{2}$$

$$F_t = M_t - X_t \tag{3}$$

where

ΔY = change in output

$\Delta K = I$ = change in capital stock or investment

S = total savings

M = total imports

X = exports

F = foreign capital inflow

t = time period t

v = incremental capital-output ratio

Substituting values from equations (2) and (3) in (1), we get

$$\Delta Y_t/Y_t = 1/v \ (S_t/Y_t + F_t/Y_t) \tag{4}$$

Equation (4) shows that as long as v is independent of S/Y and F/Y, both domestic and foreign resources have a favorable effect on growth.

Following World War II, the subject of economic growth became of great interest to economists, academics, and politicians alike. Keynesian economics had taken hold within the industrialized countries and the Harrod-Domar model had become the dominant theoretical paradigm of economic growth. This theoretical perspective, and the success of the Marshall Plan within war-torn economies, led economists to apply the Harrod-Domar model to underdeveloped countries and fueled the arguments of aid supporters who believed that foreign economic assistance would lead to economic growth. Increases in investment rates could be financed from domestic savings or from foreign resources. In fact, the Harrod-Domar model was the theoretical foundation for the first national development plans in the developing world (de Silva, 1984).

The H-D model provides the simplest possible framework within which the relationships among the aggregate macro variables can be examined. Despite its simplicity, a host of planning problems and a wide range of possibilities can be analyzed within the H-D framework. In fact, the H-D model or some variant of it is the most widely used quantitative planning technique and, even though many plan documents do not explicitly present the H-D model, elements of it can be found in the way investment requirements and the role of savings are analyzed in the formulation of the economic growth plan (Chowdhury and Kirkpatrick, 1994, p. 12).

Many development plans of low-income countries will be found to contain calculations of *savings requirements* based on these relationships (the H-D model). Development plans usually take the form of planned increases in GNP for a period of years ahead, and a model which purports to predict the amount of capital formation required to achieve given target rates of growth of GNP is naturally very attractive.   Sometimes these relationships are also used to calculate the amount of foreign aid 'required' to attain the target rates of growth. If it is manifestly impossible to achieve a rate of savings of 21 percent out of domestic income, then it is argued, the difference between the amount that can be saved and the amount of capital 'required' must be provided in the form of foreign investment or foreign aid (Elkan, 1995, p. 62).

Balanced and unbalanced growth models

During the same period in which the Harrod-Domar growth model was developed, Rosenstein-Rodan (1943), Nurske (1952) and later Hirschman (1958) also focused on the importance of savings and investment for economic growth, with particular interest on industrial investment.

Rosenstein-Rodan first wrote about a need to raise savings-investment rates in eastern and southeastern Europe to increase economic growth.   He proposed that large amounts of investment should be channeled into several industries simultaneously in order to create demand for new products (by raising worker earnings in more than one industry).   Development of manufacturing industries would require large investments over a long time period.   There would need to be simultaneous development of producer and consumer goods to utilize initial excess capacity.   The so-called "big push" idea argued that an investment push could increase the savings-investment ratio because a rapid increase in income from balanced growth would lead to a higher savings ratio out of increased incomes.   The "big push" would be in the form of government action and served as a theoretical justification for foreign aid.   According to Rosenstein-Rodan, "the purpose of an international program of aid to underdeveloped countries is to accelerate their economic development up to a point where a satisfactory rate of growth can be achieved on a self-sustaining basis" (1961, p. 107).   His ideas fit well with aid supporters because he argued that aid would be needed on a temporary basis as a stimulus to domestic capital formation.

Nurske used a similar line of reasoning to argue for a "balanced growth" approach, whereby production of a wide range of consumables would be increased to create more demand.   The idea was that only investment in a large number of activities simultaneously could take advantage of various external economies of scale.   Other versions of this balanced growth theory appear in Lewis (1955) and a sympathetic appraisal is given by Nath (1962).

Unfortunately,   the models of Rosenstein-Rodan and Nurske were interpreted by policy makers as advocating industry over agriculture, which proved disastrous in both the Soviet Union and in India (Colman and Nixon, p. 29). Other problems with the use of their models was their emphasis on capital intensive investment over labor intensive investment.   "The resources required for balanced growth are of such an order of magnitude that a country disposing of such

18

resources would in fact not be underdeveloped" (Singer, 1964, p. 46). These and other criticisms led Hirschman (1958) to advocate a model with opposite implications.

Hirschman asserted that an imbalance between supply and demand provides incentive for new projects. He argued for an "unbalanced growth" approach whereby large scale investment would be channeled by the state into only the leading industrial sector in order to "create new opportunities and bottlenecks elsewhere in the economy which would stimulate a secondary wave of investment and entreprenuership" (Colman and Nixon, p. 30). The sectors selected for investment would be evaluated in terms of their forward and backward linkages; that is, their likelihood of prompting new industries to either use their output or to supply their inputs. The sequencing of industry development was also critical. Like "big push" advocates, Hirschman accepted the need for government intervention, but this school of thought argued that a "big push" was not feasible and that development was best stimulated by creating imbalance.

Neither the balanced nor unbalanced growth models considered inherent differences between less developed countries, in terms of their objectives, resource endowments, trade prospects, population growth, etc. Neither model adequately explained the process of economic growth and development. Both were used to support arguments for the use of foreign assistance to promote economic growth in less developed countries following world War II. "These theories, emanating from the pro-aid school, were based on the general assumption that the provision of aid would lead directly to an increase in the resources available for development" (Browne, p. 105).

Rostow's stages of economic growth

Stage models of development look more generally at how the structures of economies change in the course of development (Elkan, p. 60). Like Rosenstein-Rodan, and other economists and academics of the 1940's and 1950's, Walt Rostow applied concepts from the Harrod-Domar model in his stage theory of economic growth in 1956, followed in 1960 with his book, The Stages of Growth: A Non-Communist Manifesto. As implied by the title, Rostow's book was an attempt to provide an alternative to the Marxist interpretation of history. Rostow claimed to have identified stages of economic development with which societies could be classified. The five stages were: traditional, transitional (a long period when preconditions for growth evolve), take-off (a short period toward self-sustaining growth), maturity, and high mass consumption. It was the take-off stage that incorporated Harrod and Domar's capital-output ratio and implied a significant role for aid donors. According to Rostow, there were three necessary conditions for take-off:

1   development of, and high growth in, at least one manufacturing sector;

2   a political, social and institutional framework that allows economic growth to be transmitted throughout the economy; and

3   a significant increase in investment (over ten percent of national income) (Thirlwall, 1989, p. 62).

The take-off stage was predicted to be short, with an increase in savings to 15 percent of GNP, after which time economic growth became self-sustaining. Rostow said this period would last between ten and fifteen years.

The implications for the role of aid were obvious. Rostow had described the importance of aid for development in earlier work (1957) and clearly indicated in his following book that external capital could help poor countries reach the take-off stage (Browne, p. 103). International capital markets were not directing sufficient volumes of capital to the less-developed world, and this suggested key roles for development assistance and government planning (Newark, 1995, p. 299).

By stating that investment rate increases would accelerate the process of economic growth, Rostow gave a critical role to economic aid. Through the Harrod-Domar mechanisms, investment rates could be increased with foreign capital which would raise domestic savings, without lowering domestic consumption. So aid would accelerate countries toward and through the take-off stage. The proposition that aid would only be needed on a temporary basis, after which time growth would be self-sustaining, greatly enhanced its political attractiveness for aid proponents in donor countries (Wall, 1973).

Rostow's stage theory gained wide appeal but also attracted much criticism during the 1960's. Perhaps the greatest critic was Kuznet (1963). Among Kuznet's and others' criticisms were the tautological nature of stage definitions (one can not distinguish between the end of one and the beginning of another), lack of empirical testing by Rostow, contrary quantitative evidence, and erroneous assumptions that poor countries are in the traditional stage just as developed countries used to be (ignoring historical forces that have put rich and poor countries on different paths) (Colman and Nixon, p. 39; Thirlwall, p. 62). "In practice, a recognition of uniformities in patterns of development has not proved very useful in helping to bring development about" (Elkan, p. 61). It is impossible in the history of both the developed and developing countries to identify any unique and relatively short historical phase as the period of take-off (Mikesell, 1968).

Despite the many criticisms of Rostow's and other stage theories, they continued to find supporters. According to Thirlwall, the purpose of these theories was to "distinguish the situations in which an economy may find itself" and there was no counter-argument against the important role of investment for development (p. 63). "The dominant ideas of the day emphasized that development required a concerted, deliberate, and large scale effort to break existing patterns of stagnation. These ideas included 'big push', 'take-off', and 'minimum critical effort', and all assumed a key role for an activist state in the promotion of economic development" (Newark, 1995, p. 299).

The Chenery-Strout Model

One of the most comprehensive theoretical justifications for aid, developed by Hollis Chenery and A.M. Strout in 1966, clearly followed in the footsteps of its predecessors. It is Keynesian, in that it incorporated the mechanics of the Harrod-Domar model. It is neoclassical, in that it assumed that countries tend to be self-regulatory. And it is Rostovian, in that it incorporated conditions for take-off (Browne, p. 103). Its main focus is the role of foreign savings in the growth process.

Chenery and Strout detailed how aid acted to accelerate economic development by relieving bottlenecks that constrain growth. Different types of bottlenecks were found at different stages of development, including shortages of skills, shortages of domestic savings and shortages of foreign exchange receipts. The changes needed included increased human skills, higher levels of investment and saving, more productive technology, diversification of jobs and commodities, and new societal institutions. Because in many countries there was little or no excess consumption that could be reduced to increase savings (which supports investment), foreign capital (in the form of aid or direct investment) was needed.

Foreign capital could be used to fill types of gaps that were detailed by the model and would have to fill the larger of the two gaps to avoid the bottleneck if target growth was to be achieved. Poor countries often suffer not only from savings levels below required investment levels, but from trade deficits as well. Foreign exchange meets both the savings gap and the trade gap. The savings gap determines the required financial flows as the difference between the appropriate investment level (derived from the target growth rate via a fixed capita-output ratio) and available domestic savings. In the foreign exchange gap, the size of the gap is defined as the difference between expected exports and required imports. A shortage of foreign exchange rather than insufficient domestic savings forms the bottleneck to economic development (Jepma, 1992, p. 4). "The contribution of the Chenery model is in identifying which of these gaps is the effective constraint on growth" (Chowdhury and Kirkpatrick, p. 17). When the import-export gap is larger than the investment-savings gap, saving propensities are frustrated by the inability to acquire imports for productive investment. Thus growth would be lower than what the maximum potential domestic savings would have allowed. "Herein lies, according to the two-gap model, the importance of foreign aid in the development process" (p. 21).

A total of three phases of development were outlined in the model. The stage of growth determines the character (and size) of the existing gap. During the first phase, investment levels are below the required rate to reach the target growth rate, due to a shortage of skills. During this phase, aid could fill the gap between available savings and required investment to reach targeted growth. Aid fills the gap until the rate of investment is high enough to reach the target growth rate (namely, when the domestic saving ratio rises to the level of target investment level). It was assumed that aid was not used to increase consumption by decreasing savings. So there is an investment-limited gap but not a trade-limited gap. Phase one was predicted to last between five and ten years if the investment rate averages ten to twelve percent of gross output.

During the second phase, aid is still needed because skill shortages hinder the marginal savings rate required for targeted growth (i.e., the investment rate would still be above the savings rate). It is also during this time a trade (foreign exchange) gap appears, whereby export earnings are insufficient to finance needed imports of raw materials and other factors that can not be manufactured domestically. Aid is thus needed to finance imports.

During the third phase, the investment-savings gap has disappeared but structural rigidities continue the foreign exchange gap and the need for aid. When structural changes occur and the economy adjusts to changing prices and market conditions, the phase ends (Chenery and Strout, 1966).

It is important to note the importance of domestic policies and responses in moving a country through each of the phases. In fact, the authors clearly stated that the effectiveness of external resources in contributing to economic growth was greatly influenced by the manner in which recipient countries responded. "It is the need for rapid structural change which sets the lower limit to the time required to complete the transition to self-sustaining growth" (p. 726).

In many ways Chenery and Strout echoed the sentiments of Rosenstein-Rodan. They cautioned aid supporters that the manner in which aid was used greatly determined its effectiveness. Yet the role of domestic policies in dealing with financial constraints is often ignored. They were, nonetheless, optimistic. "The general aim of aid...is to provide each underdeveloped country a positive incentive for maximum national effort to increase its rate of growth...Knowledge that capital will be available over a decade...will act in many cases as an incentive to greater effort" (Rosenstein-Rodan, 1961, p. 107). Chenery and Strout expressed that the problem of a country's inability to change its productive structure was not likely to be serious in a slowly developing country (p. 682).

Criticisms of the model include its assumption that if foreign exchange is scarce it is impossible to use domestic resources to earn more foreign exchange (non-substitutability of foreign and domestic resources), and that aid may actually substitute for domestic savings (rather than supplement it) in some cases

22

(Chowdhury and Kirkpatrick, p. 21). Other weaknesses of the early gap approach include:

1	its sensitivity to the underlying assumptions;

2	lack of clear dividing line between the contribution of official flows versus the impact of private flows;

3	its failure to deal with the impact of foreign financial inflows on domestic savings or other domestic economic variables;

4	lack of distinction between destinations and allocations of foreign financial inflows;

5	lack of consideration of interest payments on foreign debt;

6	lumping together all LDC's into one category; and

7	lack of consideration of the interdependence between recipients and the rest of the world (Jepma, pp. 6-7).

Following publication of the Chenery-Strout model, many articles began to appear in technical journals on the subject of aid and economic development. Most were not written to further develop theory but were more to test current theory with real-world evidence (Riddell, 1987, p. 92). The Chenery-Strout model continues to be a core component of development literature and is most commonly used to assess developing countries' financial requirements. Early studies of financial requirements for LDCs using the two-gap approach include: Chenery and Bruno, 1962; Adelman and Chenery, 1966; Chenery and Strout, 1966. As will be detailed in a later review of previous studies, a number of adjustments have been made to the model.

In addition to the influence of domestic policies noted by Rosenstein-Rodan, as well as by Chenery and Strout, many explanations began to emerge as to why most development programs appeared to be failing during the latter half of the 1960's. By the middle of the so-called 'development decade' of the 1960's, the United Nations reported that there had been little change or "painfully slow progress" (UN, 1966, p. 90). As noted by Zimmerman (1970), the United Nations cited many reasons for the failure of development assistance:

1	political instability;

2	indifference of the upper classes in the respective countries;

3   rapid population growth;

4   changes in disease control which lowered mortality rates without increasing standards of living;

5   unfavorable land tenure systems;

6   caste and class systems which hinder spread of knowledge among agrarianists;

7   general apathy connected with extreme poverty and/or malnutrition;

8   education or literacy;

9   suspicion of or excessive dependency upon government;

10   planning in capital cities without knowledge of or contact with local people;

11   lack of an "extension" class of persons for leadership;

12   abnegation of responsibility by governments to allow take over by outside organizations; and

13   conflict of changes with religious values (p. 4).

The concept of a "vicious cycle" became prevalent in development literature, which implied that social, political, and economic structures within the third world itself acted as the main deterrents to development (Nurske, 1953; Myrdal, 1957). The writings of liberal economic theorists made little if any connection between the development of industrialized countries and that of non-industrialized countries. The exploitative nature and impact of colonialism on the non-industrialized countries were not acknowledged (Smith, 1978; Bauer and Yancey, 1978). According to Foster-Carter (1974), no structural connection was recognized between development and underdevelopment. Development meant becoming more like the West. Thus capital, technology and skills were needed from the West, primarily via multinational corporations. Multinationals were seen as an effective vehicle to assist underdeveloped countries make better use of resources and to become developed.

Two-gap models, such as the Chenery-Strout model, focused on domestic savings and foreign exchange as alternative constraints on growth. More recently, three-gap models (such as Bacha's, 1990) have also incorporated a fiscal gap as an additional constraint on growth. This alteration was in part a response to the debt crisis of the 1980's (Agenor and Montiel, 1996, p. 427).

> There are a number of ways to incorporate the fiscal constraint in the (two-gap) model. The simplest, and most in keeping with the "two-gap" analysis, is to treat π_t (inflation) as an endogenous variable...the role of the fiscal constraint is merely to determine the rate of inflation...an increase in (net capital inflows less the sum of external debt service, transfers, and changes in foreign exchange reserves; or the foreign exchange constraint) would in this case not only serve to increase the rate of capacity growth by raising (domestic investment) (as in the two-gap approach), but would also reduce the rate of inflation by permitting the government to finance itself externally, rather than through the inflation tax...(thus) investment is determined by the available saving, foreign exchange availability, or the government budget, depending on which is the binding constraint (pp. 431-2).

Criticisms of economic growth theories

The use of economic growth theories to inform aid polices and programs has faced much criticism. Many criticisms focus on the accuracy of economic theories and models in explaining growth:

> It is not sensible to imagine that the rate of economic development of a low-income country can be mechanically related to inputs of capital alone. The national income will also be affected by the growth of entreprenuership, and by changes in attitude and institutions which favour the growth of output...In conclusion, simple macroeconomic planning models...tend to lay undue stress on the need to save in order to accumulate capital...personal saving is as likely to retard development as it is to promote it (Elkan, p. 63).

"(Development) planning represents what can be termed 'crystal ball economics'. In other words, it presupposes precise economic forecasting. However, economic performance in the Third World has never been able to achieve or even come close to the aggregates spelled out in the plans" (Hope, p. 21).

Another common criticism is that economic theories often fail to distinguish between growth and development. Bauer (1981, 1982), Krauss (1983), Lappe et al

(1980), and others, have argued that the issue of aid effectiveness lies not in whether or not aid leads to higher domestic savings or economic growth per se, but in the pattern of growth that is pursued. If aid does not effectively lower poverty levels or improve income distribution, its effect on savings levels, foreign exchange levels or growth rates are of little consequence. Real benefits from aid, they argue, have been non-existent or are marginal. Their arguments take the issue of aid effectiveness "beyond technical macroeconomic and quantifiable relationships associated with growth theory, to a consideration of quantifiable relationships that attempt to capture patterns of poverty and distribution and, relatedly, social and political aspects of the development process" (Riddell, p. 129). The issue is not so much the extent to which aid leads to economic growth, but the extent to which individual people gain or lose from the process.

> The problem of low-income countries is not how to sustain a certain rate of growth but rather how to bring changes in the economy which will make growth possible. It is a problem of *transformation* rather than of *growth*. One should not expect a theory of growth to be theory of development, since this would require an explanation of the process by which a backward economy is structurally transformed (Elkan, p. 62).

Criticisms that economic theories and models largely ignore the role of recipient governments also abound. While aid proponents have made the assumption that nation-states are able to influence and guide the development process in a way that benefits their poorest members, critics have argued, on the other hand, that recipient states are not able, or choose not, to use the process to benefit their poorest. They have argued that "internal and external forces interact to reinforce malevolent structural rigidity, thereby impeding the effect of benign social and economic forces that could lead to national development and substantial and effective poverty alleviation" (Riddell, p. 130). "Official exhortations to save, so that governments can use the proceeds to build monumental blocks of offices, probably do nothing to promote a rise in the standard of life" (Elkan, pp. 64).

Undoubtedly the greatest criticism of development economics has been its perceived ineffectiveness at achieving aims of growth or development. Lack of success in development planning based on economic theories has brought waves of dissent and a so-called 'revolution' in development orthodoxy. The change of focus in the development business is primarily been a rejection of heavy state intervention in economic planning in recipient countries. Toye (1987), and others, refer to the rejection of Keynesian economics and the resurgence of classical economics as a counter-revolution in development theory and practice (Wood, 1996, p. 32).

Since the early 1950's more than 300 different development plans have been formulated...The early enthusiasm for development planning was gradually supplanted by a growing sense of disillusionment, such that by the end of the 1970's many economists were talking openly of the 'failure of planning'...This disenchantment with development planning can be related to a number of influences. First, there was mounting evidence that actual performance often fell short of the plan targets. Second the technical limitations of the planning techniques and models being used became increasingly evident through time. Third, the dynamic growth of economies of East Asia were held up as confirmation of the superiority of a non-interventionist, market-based policy stance over the interventionist, development planning approach. The example of the Asian newly industrializing countries (NICs) in turn fueled the more general resurgence of the neoclassical paradigm in development economics, with its emphasis on the role of the price mechanism in allocating resources to their most efficient uses (Chowdhury and Kirkpatrick, pp. 2-3).

The development experience of the late 1970's and early 1980's has led to what has been called a "quiet revolution" in development thinking... This new orthodoxy promotes a development strategy that, relative to previous development fashions, foresees a drastically reduced role for the state in promoting economic development (Newark, p. 225).

The dependency theory of development

Raul Prebisch: A precursor to dependency theory

Raul Prebisch was an economist in Argentina who had served as the head of the Central Bank from 1935-1943 . He later established and became the director of the Economic Commission for Latin America (ECLA), an agency sponsored by the United Nations, in Santiago, Chile. He was one of the first development economists to question the mutual profitability of the international division of labor for developing countries. Prebisch made the first major statement of the ECLA in 1950. In his view, the world was divided into a center of industrialized countries (secondary producers) and a periphery of underdeveloped countries (primary producers). Together, the center and the periphery formed a world economic system, whereby an international division of labor relegated to the periphery the task of producing food and raw materials for the center (Prebisch, 1950). He found an unequal distribution of profits from productivity gains and different income elasticities for primary and secondary goods.

The unfavorable impact of unrestricted trade on the terms of trade and balance of payments of developing countries outweighed any advantages with respect to a more efficient allocation of resources (Thirlwall, 1989, p. 139). He urged the industrialization of the periphery, as well as trade protectionism, as a solution to disparities in development between center and periphery. This strategy became known as import-substitution industrialization. "In the view of the theorists of the (ECLA) it (was) quite possible to break out of the dependent relationship characteristics of the periphery, largely through the process of import-substitution and, at least in some degree, autonomous industrialization" (Riddell, p. 138). The substitution of imports by home production of industrial commodities for the domestic market became the official strategy of the ECLA and most of its member governments during the 1950's (Frank, 1979). As a development policy, however, it failed.

The early work of Prebisch, as well as other ECLA economists, served as a precursor to dependency approaches. Their views have been referred to as structuralism (Mahler, 1980). Generally speaking, the structuralists believed it was inevitable that primary (export) product prices, upon which less developed countries were heavily dependent, would deteriorate relative to secondary (import) product prices. Thus developed countries would gain relatively more from productivity increases for primary products, and less developed countries would continually battle with balance of payments problems and low economic growth. Regional trade organizations, preferential tariff treatment from developed countries, and import substitution (using tariffs to shelter infant industries and encouragement of foreign investment in manufacturing) were all strategies proposed by structuralists.

According to Mahler (1980), there were several key differences between structuralists and early dependency theorists. First, dependency theorists found that it was more than just the nature of the particular goods that are exchanged in global markets that leads to global inequity. Second, they were critical of structuralist support for foreign investment in periphery countries because north-south contacts are cumulative and mutually reinforcing. Third, they differed on the basic concept of development. Structuralists agreed with liberal economists that the goal of development is rapid industrialization and aggregate economic growth. Dependency theorists, on the other hand, believed that externally oriented development is distorted and seek more equitable approaches. In general, dependency theorists argued for a more fundamental change in the distribution of power between developed and less developed countries (p. 52). The central argument of structuralists became just part of the larger argument of the dependency theorists who followed them.

Dependency theorists

The dependency perspective was developed concurrently with the structuralist perspective. Three early figures were Silvio Frondizi, Sergio Bagu, and Caio

Prado Junior. All three sought socialism as a solution to the problems of underdevelopment in periphery countries (Chilcote, 1984). They found fault with imperialism and international capitalism. Dependency on monopoly capital and on multinational companies of the center was blamed for deformation of the periphery (p. 60).

The dependency perspective was brought to the English-speaking world by Andre Gunder Frank (1969, 1979). Frank developed and popularized the idea of the 'development of underdevelopment', which proposed that development and underdevelopment were part of the same process. "Underdevelopment was and still is generated by the very same historical process which also generated economic development: the development of capitalism itself" (p. 9). Poverty was said to be the "consequence of the penetration of market forces into the peripheral third world from the capitalist centre, which creates and deepens the process of underdevelopment", rather than an original state (Riddell, p. 136). The once flourishing and developed societies of Latin America, Asia, and Africa had become underdeveloped from colonization and extension of capitalist economies based in Europe. Frank criticized Rostow who had defined underdevelopment as an original stage of traditional societies, with no prior history, and proposed that developed centers were once underdeveloped. Argentina, and other countries, according to Rostow, were taking off. But Frank said they were becoming more structurally underdeveloped. Frank hypothesized (among other things) that "satellites experience their greatest economic development and especially their most classically capitalist industrial development if and when their ties to their metropolis are weakest" (1969, p. 10).

With the failure of the import-substitution strategy, a new wave of dependency theorists arose in the early 1970's and began what is now referred to as the "new dependency perspective". Much of their focus was on explaining the failure of the strategy and many of them (Cardodo, 1972; Dos Santos, 1970, 1973; Floto, 1975; Furtado, 1970; Sunkel, 1969, 1974; etc.) came from within the ECLA. They began considering more than just economics. Celse Furtado, an ECLA economist, attributed the failure of import-substitution industrialization to rigidities of the internal structure of society, traced to the Spanish conquest and Portuguese colonization. Rigid economic structures transferred to society left it resistant to social change. Therefore, the import-substitution industrialization strategy was unsuccessful. Others within the ECLA framework also looked at external relations. Theotonio Dos Santos said that import-substitution failed because a new form of dependence formed and restricted the domestic market (1973). Among the many criticisms of the import-substitution strategy were that it:

1   produced inflationary pressure;

2   limited growth to meet only domestic market demands;

3   was limited by skill shortages and inadequate infrastructure;

4   was outpaced by population growth;

5   merely shifted dependency to intermediate products; and

6   did not sufficiently distribute benefits to the poor (Furtado, 1970; Dos Santos, 1973).

According to Dos Santos (1970), there had been three forms of dependence: (1) colonialism, (2) financial-industrial (or classical dependence - Evans, 1979), and (3) new dependence from multinational corporations producing for the internal markets of dependent countries. During the first two forms of dependency, goods are produced to export to the center. Labor is super-exploited and income from exports goes abroad or to the upper class. The import-substitution industrialization strategy was attempted to diversify the industrial sector to overcome trade dependence, but a new form of dependence arose due to unavailability of investment capital. Capital from the export sector was largely foreign owned or controlled so profits went abroad. This had a negative balance of payments effect because of repatriated profits and negative terms of trade for raw materials versus industrial products. Dos Santos also offered a formal definition of dependency:

By dependency we mean a situation in which the economy of certain countries is conditioned by the development and extension of another economy to which the former is subjected. The relation of interdependence between two or more economies, and between those and world trade, assume the form of dependence when some countries (the dominant ones) can expand and be self-sustaining, while the other countries (the dependent ones) can do this only as a reflection of that expansion (1973, p. 109).

He concluded that development was a world-wide historical phenomenon from the formation, expansion and consolidation of a capitalist system; dependency, a conditioning situation that limited development and its forms.

The "new dependency perspective" differed from its older counterpart in a number of important ways. The role of foreign capital played a more central role in the new perspective. Modern dependence and underdevelopment of peripheral countries was attributed to, not only unfavorable terms of trade between primary and secondary goods, but to the penetration of foreign capital as well (primarily via the multinational corporation).

30

New dependency theorists also placed greater emphasis on the role of the internal class structure of third world countries than had their predecessors. The upper class of the third world was said to be part of a transnational community of the affluent who consume and live in ways common among the middle classes of developed countries (Sunkel, 1974). The upper class served as a link between the country and multinational corporations by forming joint ventures.

Thus new dependency theory put foreign capital investors and the internal class structure into the limelight of the development controversy. Development could occur, according to this perspective, despite dependence on the core; but it was limited, was not self-generating, and was not likely to distribute benefits evenly to a majority of the population.

Criticisms of dependency theory in general include that: (1) it is static in its formulations, especially regarding the role of external forces (O'Brien, 1975, p. 24; Lall, 1975, p. 800; Warren, 1980, p. 165), which implies that definitions are tautological or meaningless; and (2) the theory does not fit the facts (Lall, 1975), in that industrial countries have a high penetration of foreign capital too and because some former colonies have actually done well (such as some Asian countries, Argentina, and Brazil).

Dependency theory has made a lasting contribution to the debate and understanding of the development process and the importance of domestic and foreign forces within the process. It is now widely acknowledged that the process by which some countries have become more advanced has led to the opposite outcome for others. The basic tenets of dependency theory have carried through into the World System perspective, whereby national societies are hierarchically positioned within a larger world division of labor.

The best proponent of the World System perspective is Immanuel Wallerstein who traced the development of capitalism since the sixteenth century (Wallerstein, 1974a, 1980). He identified the world system as a social system with a single division of labor: "a world economy with territorially defined division of labor organized as a set of competing political entities with unequal power" (1974a, p. 222). Individual nations' prosperity is determined by political and economic power. No one nation can maintain control over the economy of the entire system.

Wallerstein proposed that the world was divided into not two, but three tiers: the core, periphery and semi-periphery. Core countries have diversified and well-integrated economies with complex internal division of labor and high productivity in manufacturing and agriculture. A relatively free, high-wage skilled labor force is the primary form of labor exploitation. In the periphery, there is a dualistic economic structure with a modern export sector of raw materials and a traditional sector of villages and remote areas where labor is recruited for the modern sector. Labor is relatively unskilled, with low wages or is politically coerced. Some areas are better linked to the outside than to other internal areas.

Also, a semi-periphery exists with core and periphery characteristics, that trades with both. It is the exploited and the exploiter. The semi-periphery is not residual but holds a functional position. It is in the process of moving up or down in the system. It provides political stability so the exploited do not unite in opposition (Wallerstein, 1974b). Reproduction of the core-periphery division of labor has resulted in upward and downward mobility for individual countries. The semi-periphery allows industrialization to occur outside the core without eliminating the basic core-periphery hierarchy.

Economic aid from the dependency perspective

Most Latin American dependency theorists focused on foreign direct investment, not aid, for the underdevelopment of the periphery. However, a number of dependency theorists, and aid critics outside of the dependency school, have offered discussion on both general and specific means by which aid impacts negatively on the development of periphery countries. Some of the most common criticisms of aid are outlined below.

Restrictions and conditions placed on aid prevent it from substituting for any domestic economic surplus which is drained from the periphery to the core due to foreign control of export sectors and capital deficits. Aid is often used to introduce ill-suited technology, to subsidize imports that compete with domestic products, or to finance foreign investment in low priority sectors (Dos Santos, 1970). Aid is often used on projects that attract foreign investment, such as roads and schools, rather than on projects that help create domestic industries. Much aid is 'tied' to donor goods that are often over-priced (Frank, 1969). Aid is also often in the form of loans, rather than grants, that must be repaid in foreign exchange from export earnings. The result may be over-specialization in export industries, rather than domestic industries (Szymanski, 1981). Aid lowers the domestic marginal propensity to save which distorts domestic capital formation (Griffin, 1970). Agricultural or food aid may disrupt domestic production, distribution and land tenure, which leaves a country more dependent on aid than before (Lappe et.al., 1980; Linear, 1985).

Aid has also been described as a new form of imperialism that maintains political and economic control over periphery countries. It is used to increase military presence and to ensure free access to raw materials and trade for donor countries. Donor countries influence the conditionality of policies of multilateral organizations so that any economic development in the periphery will be capitalistic and dependent upon investment capital. Bilateral and multilateral organizations often make aid conditional on policies to 'stabilize' the economy that are designed to maintain trade patterns and flows of foreign investment, to continue debt payments and to build a social and economic system resistant to revolutionary change (Hayter, 1971, 1981; Hayter and Watson, 1985; McNeill,

1981; Szymanski, 1981; Carty and Smith, 1985). In essence, aid is a tool of deception that allows exploitation of the masses in the name of 'assistance' (Jalle, 1968; Hayter, 1971, 1981, 1985; Magdoff, 1969).

In general, criticisms of aid from the dependency perspective, and other perspectives, are that it:

1   distorts periphery economies;

2   attracts and supports foreign-owned industries over domestic industries;

3   helps to maintain a capitalistic system on a world-wide scale; and

4   suppresses autonomous policies of governments to control their own economies.

Robert Wood (1980, 1986) describes how these things occur via an "international aid regime" that operates at the world level. The regime is designed to ensure continual dominance of core economies over peripheral economies by exerting influence over government policies within recipient countries. Four aspects of the foreign aid regime limit control of aid and thus exert influence on government policies: (1) the negotiation framework; (2) strategic non-lending; (3) institutionalized non-competition; and (4) emphasis on social and physical infrastructure rather than on industrial development (Baldwin, 1965; Wood, 1980, 1986).

Mercantilist theory of development

A brief review of mercantilism serves to highlight another perspective on world economic order and economic development. Mercantilism can be easily contrasted with the dependency perspective in that the role of the nation-state is viewed as the future's most powerful influence on international capital flows, rather than the multinational corporation. As described by Gilpin (1971),

In the dependencia model...the flow of wealth and benefits is seen as moving from the global, underdeveloped periphery to the centers of industrial financial power and decision...In the interdependent world economy of the dependencia model, the multinational corporation reigns supreme...(In) the mercantilist view, the interdependent world economy, which has provided such a favorable environment for the multinational corporation, is coming to an end...The mercantilist model views the nation-state and the interplay of national interests

33

(as distinct from corporate interests) as the primary determinants of the future role of the economy (pp. 43-5).

The terms mercantilism (Gilpin, 1975), neomercantilism (Bergstein et.al., 1978), organic statism (Stepan, 1978), and nation-state independence theory (Braungart and Braungart, 1981) have all been used to describe this perspective. Their distinction from other perspectives or theories of development is the importance they place on domestic factors, particularly state policy, as the center of analysis. This was not the case in either liberal economic theory, nor dependency theory. Gilpin defines mercantilism as "the attempt of governments to manipulate economic arrangements in order to maximize their own interests, whether or not this is at the expense of others...a far broader (definition) than its eighteenth-century association with a trade and balance of payments surplus" (p. 45).

The role of foreign capital is in opposition to, and by its nature a challenge to, the nation-state (Stepan, 1978), a view not dissimilar to dependency theorists. However, nation-states have and will continue to have the power to limit the "disintegrative effects" of foreign capital and to use their resources to better meet the social and economic needs of their citizens (a view more similar to liberal economic theory). Bergsten (1975), Keohane and Ooms (1975), and Stepan (1978) found overestimation of the power of multinational corporations (to help or hinder development efforts) in other theories of development.

Thus it would seem that when testing the impact of foreign aid (and other forms of foreign capital) on economic growth, three very different outcomes would be predicted by the theories reviewed here: (1) Liberal economic theory would generally predict a positive relationship between foreign capital and growth; (2) Dependency theory would predict a negative relationship; (3) Mercantilism would have no prediction because the issue is not amount of foreign capital penetration but the effectiveness of nation-state policies to control and capitalize on its impact.

4 Review of Previous Studies

Econometricians and sociologists were the first to examine the relationship between aid and economic growth using statistical techniques during the 1960's. Many studies have followed, with little unanimity on the conclusions. A review of earlier studies from both the perspective of economic theory and alternative perspectives is necessary to discern the reason(s) for the lack of consensus regarding the effectiveness of aid in contributing to economic growth in recipient countries.

Economic studies of aid effectiveness

Early to mid-1960's

The earliest studies of aid effectiveness using economic theory typically used the Harrod-Domar model. Among the best known studies were Rosenstein-Rodan (1961), Chenery and Bruno (1962), Chenery and Adelman (1966), and Chenery and Strout (1966). The independent variable in these studies was total resource inflow. Aid was assumed to be a large component of the flow, and was assumed to directly contribute to capital stock. The capital-output ratio of recipient countries was assumed to be stable. From these assumptions, a country (with a growth rate determined by the quotient of its marginal propensity to save (S) and its incremental capital-output ratio (v)) would raise its growth rate from (S/v) to $(S+a)/v$, where a is aid as a fraction of GNP. Thus inflows were assumed to only increase investment.

With the 1966 development of the Chenery-Strout model, numerous studies began to appear that tested the model and its assumptions. One of the first studies was Rahman's (1968) test of the savings-growth relationship and the Chenery-Strout savings-gap assumptions. Rahman took an earlier suggestion from Trygve Haavelmo (1963) that domestic savings was not a function of income alone but was also related inversely with foreign capital inflow, and tested it more formally. He used Haavelmo's hypothesis, which indicates that the savings function of the less developed country is:

$$I_t = a\,(Y_t + H_t)\,,$$

where I stands for gross investment; Y for gross national product; H for capital flows. That is to say that investment...is a function of...income, including what they get from abroad...Domestic savings is not a function of national income alone, but also related inversely to inflows of foreign capital (Rahman, 1968, p. 137).

Rahman used the same cross-sectional data used by Chenery and Strout (for 31 countries in 1962) and ran ordinary least squares (OLS) regression of the savings ratio on the ratio of capital inflows to GNP. Rahman maintained that Haavelmo's hypothesis might be right, a behaviorist hypothesis that governments in developing countries may "voluntarily relax domestic savings efforts when more foreign aid is available than otherwise" (Rahman, p. 317). He interpreted this as "insight into the behavior of recipients of foreign capital that is yet to be recognized, especially by those who postulate domestic savings to be a function only of national income, with the presumption that foreign capital is used only for augmenting investment and not as a substitute for domestic savings" (p. 138). Rahman's conclusions were only the first of many to come that would challenge the assumptions of the Chenery-Strout model.

Tests of the model were also performed in 1970 by Keith Griffin, and by Griffin and J.L. Enos (1970). It was also Griffin's intention to counter the savings-gap portion of the Chenery-Strout model which advocated that foreign aid promotes economic growth. Griffin proposed that aid is essentially a substitute for savings and that a large fraction of foreign capital is used to increase consumption rather than investment. He referred to the issue as 'fungibility' of aid. This opposed the Chenery-Strout model which was based on the assumption that any increase in foreign capital is devoted entirely to raising the rate of capital accumulation. To demonstrate his theoretical contention that foreign aid might reduce domestic savings, he produced some single equation regression results based on cross-section data and on time-series data for a single country. Griffin believed his study was the first of its kind and cautioned that it was based on data of poor quality.

Nonetheless, from an OLS regression analysis of 32 underdeveloped countries, from 1962-64, and other empirical evidence cited from the Organization of American States (1968), N.H. Leff (1968), and Colin Clark (date not given), Griffin concluded that aid had not contributed to economic growth and was associated with a drop in savings. A number of reasons were proposed: aid may be biased in favor of capital-intensive technology which raises the capital-output ratio and the need for more capital; aid may lead to diversion of government funds from investment toward social programs or to lower taxes; aid may lower private domestic savings. His main conclusions were:

1   Foreign capital represents a transfer of resources or purchasing power from one country to another.

2   Foreign capital (aid included) will alter the composition of the investment in such a way that the marginal capital output ratio will be larger.

3   Capital imports would tend to increase the rate of growth by much less than orthodox models would suggest (Griffin, 1970, pp. 101-112).

With Enos, Griffin again intended to disprove some of the assumptions and predictions of previous literature.

Our thesis is that not all help is helpful; not all aid assists...(if) the growth which   a nation achieves, or fails to achieve, is related to the assistance it receives, one finds that there is no support for the view that aid encourages growth (Griffin and Enos, 1970).

Again data availability was a constraint and the authors cautioned that "our method (is) largely unscientific and suggestive rather than assertive" (p. 313). A bivariate regression analysis of the average rate of growth of GNP on the ratio of foreign aid to GNP was performed on 15 African and Asian less developed countries from 1962-64. The result was a non-significant association between aid and growth. An OLS regression analysis on 12 Latin American countries from 1957-64 found a significantly negative association between aid and growth. By their interpretation, aid not only did not help growth, it could lower growth. It was their conclusion that an extra dollar of aid is associated with a rise in consumption of about 75 cents and a rise in investment of only about 25 cents.

Aid and domestic savings are substitute resources, and therefore, the pattern of development is complex and the effect of foreign assistance is still underestimated. But it is clear that the relationship usually assumed to exist between aid and growth is too simple; in general, foreign assistance has neither accelerated growth nor helped to foster democratic political regimes. If anything, aid may have retarded development by leading to lowered domestic savings, by distorting the consumption of investment, and thereby raising the capital output ratio, by frustrating the emergence of an indigenous entrepreneurial class and by inhibiting institutional reform (Griffin and Enos, 1970, p. 326).

Griffin and Enos disputed the assumption that foreign aid relieves a country's savings constraint, thereby permitting and encouraging a country to invest more in capital goods than its domestic savings rate would ordinarily allow. This assumption is a major part of the foundation of the "two-gap" model of growth from Chenery and Strout (Over, 1975).

The following year several comments on Griffin's work were published. Kennedy and Thirlwall (1971) commented that:

Griffin's conclusions about the effects of foreign aid on economic development and domestic savings is inaccurate because Griffin's analysis assumes that the LDC's are subject to only one constraint on investment, vs. savings. They reject the alternative proposition that foreign exchange can be an independent constraint on development...Griffin is careful not to rest his argument (i.e., substitutability between capital imports and domestic savings) exclusively on the statistical evidence, since he admits that the negative sign of the regression coefficient could have various interpretations. In our view, he rejects too hastily the explanation that countries receive aid because they save a low proportion of their national income (pp. 135-7).

They also criticized Griffin because he improperly defined aid as the deficit on the current account of the balance of payments, and he improperly hypothesized that some capital-intensive projects affect the overall capital-output ratio for the entire economy and so concludes that foreign capital may actually reduce growth rates. Frances Stewart leveled similar criticisms, adding, "Such crude cross country analysis cannot be treated seriously" (p. 142). On his own behalf, Griffin noted his critics but countered that they had provided no empirical evidence. "If nothing else, we should be able to agree that there is a problem to be explained" (p. 157).

Challenges to at least part of the Chenery-Strout model from Rahman and Griffin were continued in a 1972 study by Thomas Weisskopf. His objective was to "test the hypothesis that the level of domestic savings in underdeveloped countries is behaviorally related not only to the level of national income, but also to the level of net foreign capital inflow...there is a theoretical reason for believing that inflows of foreign capital should have a negative impact on the domestic intention to save" (p. 25). Weisskopf employed a model consisting of seven equations in nine variables, and three inequality constraints (which were emphasized in the two-gap literature). Results from time series data for at least seven years with 44 underdeveloped countries were consistent with those of Rahman and Griffin and Enos, who also found a negative relationship between foreign aid and economic development. Weisskopf concluded:

> The impacts of foreign capital inflows on ex ante domestic savings in underdeveloped countries is significantly negative, to an extent that varies from one country to another. Foreign savings appear to have been substituted for domestic savings...Therefore, the negative impact of foreign capital inflows on domestic saving applies ex ante, but not necessarily to ex post savings. Only in countries characterized by a binding savings constraint and slack trade constraints is the relationship between foreign capital and ex post savings described by the ex ante savings function. When the trade constraint is active, the impact of foreign inflows on ex post savings is more likely to be positive (p. 37).

In sum, most researchers during this phase seemed to agree that aid and other inflows reduced domestic savings and were used in part to increase consumption. Some also argued that aid and foreign investment had negative social and political consequences as well. Among the most common criticisms of aid was that it was biased in favor of capital-intensive technology, had a tendency to increase subsequent need for capital, prejudiced exports, raised capital-output ratios, and decreased economic growth.

Mid 1970's

The methodology used by earlier researchers came under attack in the literature and studies of the mid 1970's. Previous researchers had used aggregate measures of aid and other inflows and had inferred a causal relationship from aid to savings. After correcting for these and other problems, some third phase researchers found a positive correlation between aid and growth.

The aid-savings-growth pendulum swung in this direction with a 1975 study by A. Mead Over Jr. Over began by praising Griffin and Enos with a "refreshingly atypical examination of the sociopolitical surroundings of foreign aid whose net effect on this resource flow may turn it to the detriment of the recipient country" (p. 751). However, Over observed that the regression equation Griffin and Enos tested (whereby savings is a function of foreign aid plus the residual) was only half of a two-equation model.

The Griffin-Enos approach assumed that aid donations were not determined by the gap between necessary investment levels and insufficient savings levels, but rather according to donor interests (i.e., they assumed aid to be exogenous, meaning the aid coefficient and the error term are independent). Over found this assumption to be naïve and concluded that their use of ordinary least squares was inappropriate because aid was not independent of the error term (i.e., aid was more likely determined by savings-investment gap). He argued that domestic investment, not foreign aid, should be treated as exogenous. It is this change in the assumption that domestic investment is exogenous that makes the use of OLS method inappropriate for the model of Griffin and Griffin and Enos. Over replicated the Griffin-Enos study, using the same data but two-stage least squares rather than ordinary least squares regression. In the system of equations, aid was first taken as a function of investment levels; then savings was taken as a function of the fitted aid values from the first equation.

Over found that, contrary to Griffin and Enos' (as well as Weisskopf's) conclusions, his re-estimation "firmly support(ed) the argument that aid complements growth - and even elicits an additional matching increase in the domestic savings rate" (p.755). In the end, however, he cautioned that the raw data is "meager", the model is "primitive", and it is impossible to draw any conclusions about the more likely savings-aid-growth relationship. Griffin and Enos (1975) countered that aid should be treated as exogenous to a recipient country because its allocation is determined more by political factors in the lending country than by recipient country needs.

Papanek (1972) also criticized Griffin's view that aid leads to increased consumption instead of domestic savings. In Papanek's view, one can not say there is a causal relationship and can not say that aid is the most important cause of declining savings. He characterized previous essays that criticized foreign aid as 'revisionist' and found them lacking any specifics about the savings function that underlies their assumed relationship. Papanek believed that almost all inflow (from aid and foreign direct investment) is directly invested, so income and savings rise. In any case, he concluded, there must be some benefit from an increase in investment due to inflows, even if consumption also rises. Negative statistical relationships between savings and foreign inflow, he argued, could be partly attributed to an accounting convention and may not be a behavioral relationship. Papanek also criticized Griffin for his measurement of aid and his exclusion of other factors, such as political turmoil, weather, terms of trade, influence of religion and culture on society, etc. Griffin's measurement of capital inflows should have been broken into private investment, aid, and other foreign inflows, according to Papanek.

Papanek estimated the separate effect of inflows on growth in 1973. First he modified the Chenery-Strout model, eliminating the assumption that inflows affect growth through savings. Instead, he said inflows and savings are independent variables that explain growth. And whereas Griffin and Enos used deficit on current account as a measure of aid, Papanek distinguished between different types of capital flows. Instead of treating all capital inflows as a single group, he disaggregated them into three parts: foreign aid, foreign private investment, and all other inflows. He used a cross-sectional study of 34 countries in the 1950's and 51 countries in the 1960's. One of his single equation models is of the form $Y = f(S, AID, FIP, RFI)$, where Y denotes growth in GDP; S is gross domestic savings; AID is foreign aid received and long term borrowings made by the government; FPI is foreign private investment; and RFI is other foreign inflows, all of which are expressed as percentages of GDP. He found that all three flows (aid, foreign private investment, and other foreign inflows) had a statistically significant positive effect on growth, and the effect from aid on growth was more significant than other factors. In fact, for all the countries combined the AID variable explained forty percent of the increase in output. Also, he considered export rates, education, size of the manufacturing sector, and population, but found effects that were not significant.

By the mid-1970's aid effectiveness research had been altered in three important ways: (1) The use of total foreign capital inflows as a measure for aid was found to be improper; (2) Control for domestic capital formation became necessary when assessing the effects of other factors; and (3) The Chenery-Strout model was permanently modified (allowing that aid may increase consumption instead of increasing savings).

Chenery found that by the mid 1970's as much as half of external resources had gone to increase consumption (Chenery and Syrquin, 1975). Chenery agreed that the Chenery-Strout model should be modified because not all of foreign capital inflows go to investment, and aid could be directed toward increased consumption (Chenery, 1979). "Although most studies found a negative relationship between domestic savings and foreign aid, only a few found that the coefficient of the foreign capital variable was less than minus unity and that foreign capital reduced total savings. Thus while a portion of foreign capital is used for consumption and may substitute for domestic savings, the remainder augments capital formation and growth" (Ahmed, 1992, p. 80).

In 1975 Colin Stoneman tested a "new but simple model of the impact of foreign capital on the economic growth rate of poor countries". Stoneman described the impetus for his study as the "inappropriately narrow viewpoint" of related investigations (by Griffin, Griffin and Enos, Weisskopf, Papanek, and others). Stoneman criticized his predecessors for failing to distinguish between two main effects from foreign direct investment: (1) the balance of payments effect (inflows of capital enable higher investment and consumption); and (2) effects on the structure of the economy (foreign inflows induce export promotion, change the capital-output ratio, affect income distribution, etc.). One of the major differences between Stoneman and Papanek was related to the measurement of the variables, such as domestic savings and private direct foreign investment. They did agree, however, on the positive relationship between aid and economic growth.

41

Stoneman rejected the "orthodox theorists", such as Griffin, Enos, Weisskopf, and Rahman.

Stoneman performed ordinary least squares regression analysis for five year periods between 1955 and 1970 on a main sample of 188 countries, and several sub-samples, using the following independent variables: gross domestic investment, net inflow on direct investment account, net inflow of foreign aid and other foreign long-term flows, and the stock of foreign direct investment. The dependent variable was annual average growth in GDP. His results "confirm(ed) the favorable impact of aid flows and domestic savings (on economic growth), but suggest(ed) that direct investment is associated with structural effects that retard growth" (p.11). His conclusion was weakened somewhat by the lack of significance for any specific geographical region. Stoneman made an important note that, like his predecessors, his model assumed a linear relationship between each of the variables and growth. "That is we can offer no opinion on the possibility that there is an initially favorable impact of foreign investment on growth, say up to twenty percent of GNP, after which further domination has a negative effect" (p. 18).

The 1980's

Mosely (1980) also desegregated capital inflows, and in addition lagged foreign capital inflows by five years. With a sample of 83 countries and the time period of 1970-77, Mosley performed a two-stage least squares regression with the following variables: (1) In the first equation, level of development was the dependent variable and the independent variables were savings, aid, and other foreign capital inflows; (2) In the second equation, aid was the dependent variable and level of development was the independent variable. Thus he hypothesized that aid influenced and was influenced by a country's level of income. The effect of aid and other inflows on growth were not significant, except for the 30 poorest countries where aid was significantly positive.

The use of level of development, rather than rate of economic growth, was a "curious substitution" in the Chenery-Strout model wherein aid influences growth, not income level (Lockwood, 1990). Also, in his second equation, he implies that level of development affects aid. Yet aid was lagged for a time period before the level of development figure.

Islam (1982) conducted a multivariate study of the role of foreign economic influence and domestic growth factors in the development process. Cross-sectional and longitudinal data analysis procedures were utilized for 1976 and from 1960-76 respectively, for 78 third world countries. A total of 18 indicators were used (seven to cover the broad definition of development). The principal findings concerned the role of foreign economic influences on third world development, the effects of domestic growth factors on foreign investment, the influence of domestic growth factors on development, and the predictive power of the development theories. Islam found that the effect of foreign economic influence on development was negative and that "when all relationships are considered the theory that is best supported by these findings is the old dependency theory" (p. 337).

Dowling and Hiemenz (1983) commented that the question of aid effectiveness for economic development was gaining new prominence and had been the source of "vigorous debate" since the early 1970's. However, a ten-year neglect in the literature had arisen, according to Papanek (1983), not because the controversy had disappeared, but because of "general boredom with the whole issue of economic development" (p. 171).

The intention of Dowling and Hiemenz was to offer a counter-argument to their predecessors who found no general relationship between aid, savings, and growth. They focused exclusively on the Asian region to suggest that a significant and positive relationship existed between aid and economic growth during the seventies. They performed ordinary least squares regression, using the "standard explanatory variables" (aid, capital inflows, and savings), plus four policy variables. Their sample covered 52 countries of the Asian region over the period of 1968-79, in three year periods.

All three standard variables were found to be positively and significantly related to growth. "These results strongly support the hypothesis that foreign aid contributes to economic growth and are roughly consistent with similar conclusions drawn by Papanek from an analysis of data drawn in the 1960's...and contradict Mosley's recent pessimistic estimates" (pp. 7, 11). They also cautioned against any suggestions that they should have used the two-stage least squares approach. "The alleged bias in the least squares estimate of the coefficient on foreign aid arises because of the feedback between aid and the level of GDP...not between the growth rate in GDP and aid. There is no obvious reasons why the rate of growth in GDP and the level of GDP/capita should be highly correlated at any point in time" (p. 8).

Gupta and Islam (1983) used data on 52 developing countries for the time periods 1950-60 and 1964-73 and used two types of sample disaggregation (by income group and by geographic region). They specified and estimated a simultaneous equations model in which both the savings rate and the growth rate affect each other (where savings is a positive function of growth and growth is a positive function of savings). Their major findings included that domestic savings as well as foreign capital made a significant contribution to growth but that the former is relatively more important than the latter. Also, single equation models overestimate the effect of foreign capital on growth because they do not capture the indirect impact via domestic savings. As for the disaggregation of foreign capital, the results suggest a slight advantage of foreign aid over foreign private investment but there is a trade-off. While foreign private investment has a less adverse effect on domestic savings than aid, aid makes a more significant contribution to growth.

An in-depth examination of the effects of foreign capital infusions into the Egyptian economy during the period of 1967-83 was the purpose of Abou-Setteit's 1986 study. Foreign capital was broken into foreign aid, foreign investment and private unrequited transfers. From OLS regression in a time series model, foreign aid and private unrequited transfers were found to accelerate the growth rates of GNP and capital formation, while foreign investment retarded both. Foreign aid also increased the growth rate of public investments. "These positive effects were attributed to a relaxation of the foreign exchange and investment constraints. The negative effects of foreign investments were ascribed to the preponderant allocation of these resources to consumption oriented services" (p. 180).

In 1987, Mosley continued his study of aid as 'an instrument of development'. As part of a fairly comprehensive investigation of aid effectiveness, Mosley considered whether aid effectiveness had changed over time and what factors were responsible for those changes. Mosley noted that he and his predecessors (by using aid plus savings plus other inflows determine growth equations) were in essence using a simple Harrod-Domar growth model, with investment divided into three components according to the source of finance: aid, commercial inflows from overseas, or domestic savings. It was his contention that this model was over-simplified and should also include changes in skills (literacy growth rates) and growth of export values.

As in his previous study, Mosley chose to lag aid and other foreign inflows, but this time by seven years (rather than five). His analysis included ordinary least squares, two-stage least squares, and the Cochrane-Orcutt iterative procedure, for three time periods from 1960-83. From OLS, aid had no significant relationship with growth, for the entire sample of 67 countries and for sub-samples. Only export growth retained significance throughout the 20 year period. Mosley attributed the difference in results between he and Papanek, in part, to different data sets. They also used different measures of aid, different lag structures and a different set of independent variables alongside aid. Under both two-stage least squares (wherein aid is also a function of growth) and the Cochrane-Orcutt iterative method of estimation, aid flows remained non-significant as a determinate of GNP growth.

With John Hudson and Sara Horrell, Mosley (1987) summarized theoretical literature as:

> clear that if the giving of aid to a poor country depressed the savings rate or raises its capital-output ratio...there is a possibility that aid may 'immiserise' the recipient. The empirical literature suggests that this theoretical possibility has not yet materialized, in the sense that the partial regression coefficient of aid on

growth is reported to be significant and positive for both the 1960's and the 1970's (p. 616).

They extended Mosley's earlier two-stage model into a three equation system (using the same data and time periods). In the first equation, growth is a function of aid, other financial flows, savings, literacy growth and export growth. In the second equation, aid is a function of beginning per capita income, beginning mortality rate, and a dummy variable for OPEC and Arab League countries. The third equation represents change in mortality as a function of aid, beginning per capita income, and growth. The results were that aid flows were correlated with level of income, but not with growth. Aid shifted from negative to positive but was not significant. They concluded that:

it (is) impossible to establish any statistically significant correlation between aid and the growth rate of GNP in developing countries...The apparent inability of development aid over more than twenty years to provide a net increment to overall growth in the Third World must give the donor community, as it gives us, cause for grave concern (p. 616).

Essuman (1987) conducted a cross-section statistical analysis of the aid-growth relationship in Sub-Saharan Africa over the period of 1975-84. The OLS method was used to estimate the aid equation while the two-stage least squares criterion was used for the estimation of the growth equation for 37 countries. The overall results indicated that the significant and positive relationship between aid and growth which Papanek reported for the 1960's had collapsed during the 1975-84 period. The results did confirm Mosely's (1980) findings of a weak and insignificant but negative correlation between aid and growth. And the results confirmed the findings of Griffin and Enos (1970) that there is a strong and significantly negative correlation between aid and savings (thought not necessarily a causal relationship). His results were consistent with the hypothesis that aid effectiveness varies over time, and from country to country. "Generally, there are no conclusive answers to the relationship between aid and growth" (p. 307).

In 1988 the study of foreign capital and its impact on economic growth of developing countries remained controversial (Rana and Dowling). Pradumna Rana and J. Malcolm Dowling Jr. summarized the results of previous studies as generally supporting that foreign capital is a partial substitute for domestic saving (Rahman, Griffin and Enos, Papanek, Weisskopf, etc.) but nevertheless a positive contributor to economic growth (Papanek, Stoneman, Dowling and Hiemenz, etc.). Among their criticisms of earlier studies were that growth performance should include domestic savings, foreign capital, and export performance as explanatory variables; while foreign capital, per capita income, growth rate and export performance are important determinants of savings. Also, previous studies "considered only the direct effects of exogenous variables...Total effects (direct plus indirect) could, therefore, be quite different from direct effects alone" (p. 4).

They tested a simple two-equation model: (1) growth = aid + foreign private investment + savings + export growth + change in labor force; and (2) savings = aid + foreign private investment + export growth + GDP per capita + GDP growth. The two-equation model was estimated by the indirect least squares technique. The data was pooled cross-section and time-series data from nine developing Asian countries during 1965-82 using three year averages. The model was then estimated by the Fuller Battese technique. Foreign investment and growth of labor force were positively and significantly related to growth. From the second equation, only per capita GDP was statistically significant in its relationship with savings.

> The major finding of the paper is that foreign capital flows have made a positive contribution to the growth of Asian developing countries. While foreign direct investment has contributed to growth both by augmenting resources available for capital formation and by improving investment efficiency, foreign aid has contributed only by aiding in capital formation (p. 9).

Akef (1988) conducted an empirical study of the impact of foreign economic aid on investment in Egypt and examined the productivity of aid to Egypt from 1960-84. He used the two-gap approach to measure productivity in order to determine which gap was constraining Egyptian development. He concluded that aid to Egypt during the period did not support domestic resources, but supplemented them; the level of development of the recipient country has a significant impact on the efficient use of aid; the savings rate decreased after adopting the open door economic policy; leakage of aid was more than 50 percent (about 57 percent of aid was spent on consumption and government expenditures); and the savings gap was the constraining gap in the economy (pp. 113-4).

A 1989 study by Jacques Morisset focused exclusively on the relationship between foreign capital inflows and domestic savings in Argentina. Previous studies were criticized for not specifying the savings function which underlies the foreign capital flows-domestic savings relationship, and for assuming a causal relationship between the two. "Empirical results may actually be a consequence of exogenous factors, and therefore the econometric results should not be systematically interpreted as the impact of foreign capital inflows on domestic savings" (p. 1709). A savings function for Argentina was derived from economic theory and literature. The short-run savings function indicated that savings was a function of GDP, foreign capital inflows, the real interest rate, the inflation rate, and consumption. Results from OLS (1960-81) did not support the substitution hypothesis which assumes that foreign capital crowds out savings by allowing domestic residents to consume more. "We can conclude that the mid-specification of the savings function in previous studies resulted in over-estimating the impact of foreign capital on savings for Argentina" (p. 1713).

The 1990's

In 1990, Daniel Landau used the 'public choice approach' to study aid effectiveness. The approach applies the same basic assumption that is used in the study of consumers and producers to public decision makers. "Decision makers in the public sector are assumed to be trying to maximize their personal benefits similarly to consumers and firms" (p. 559). His hypothesis was that governments would be motivated by aid to reallocate resources to create more transfers/rents, which would limit aid effectiveness but would not slow economic growth. Growth rates were calculated in five, seven, nine, eleven and thirteen year averages for 63 less developed countries. Independent variables included growth rate of world GDP, lagged level of per capita income, enrollment rates in three levels of education, share of government expenditure on goods and services, aid, and population growth rate. "The results are consistent with the hypothesis. The coefficient for aid changes markedly in the positive direction when government consumption expenditure is held constant" (p. 565). Their conclusions were as follows: (1) aid is used directly on projects that further economic growth; (2) growth-promoting effects of aid are negated by reaction of recipient governments to increase rent/transfer-creating government activities. However, they cautioned that the statistical results were not strong and "there are a myriad of reasons why further research could overturn these modest results" (p. 565).

The trio of Mosley, Hudson and Horrell continued their study of the matter and published "Aid Effectiveness and Policy" in 1992. They offered an important reminder that:

despite bleak macro evidence on the performance of aid so far, all prescriptions...concur in recommending that problems can be eased only if there is an increase in aid flows. It is urgent to ascertain whether this represents a potentially meaningful strategy, or simply the triumph of hope over experience (p. 170).

Their study differed from its predecessors in a number of ways: (1) It used data for most of the 1980's; (2) It explicitly addressed the impact of policy regime on aid effectiveness; and (3) It examined changes in aid effectiveness status between decades to look for a pattern in the changes.

They began with an OLS regression analysis of possible determinants of GDP growth rate (aid, other inflows, savings, exports, literacy, and a policy openness dummy variable) using a nine year average for the 1980-88 time period on 71 developing countries. Aid and other foreign inflows were lagged by seven years. Aid was found to be positive and significant ("for the first time according to our measurements"), as well as savings and export growth; other inflows and the policy openness dummy variable were positive but not significant.

Next they split the scatter of aid and growth observations into four quadrants (divided by growth and the aid/growth ratio), labeled high aid-high growth, high aid-low growth, low aid-high growth, and low aid-low growth. The quadrants represented 'stages of aid effectiveness' through which countries move from near-subsistence levels (low aid-low growth) to graduation out of the need for aid (low aid-high growth) in a counter-clockwise manner over time. The existence of countries in all four quadrants simultaneously, they hypothesized, could explain the often non-significant aid coefficients found in linear regression tests. Admittedly the model ignored the non-aid influences on growth that were controlled for in the regression analysis. Nonetheless, they compared the first set of results by quadrant with a second set of quadrants for the time period of 1970-80 to find if indeed countries had progressed in a counter-clockwise manner. They found that counter-clockwise movement dominated clockwise movement from one decade to the next. Particular attention is needed, they noted, for those countries that moved in a clockwise manner.

Also in 1992, Ahmed conducted an econometric analysis regarding the macroeconomic contribution of foreign aid on economic growth and domestic savings in the Bangladesh economy. In order to assess the impact of aid on savings, a simultaneous-equations model of growth and savings was chosen and estimated for the 1972-91 period. In the first equation, growth rate of GDP was a function of aid, foreign private investment, domestic savings, changes in exports and changes in the labor force (the traditional export augmented neoclassical production function). In the second equation, savings was a function of aid, foreign private investment, changes in exports, GDP per capita, and the growth rate of GDP (the traditional Keynesian-type savings function augmented by the export variable, per capita income and GDP growth rate). The results indicated that foreign aid was inversely related with the growth of GDP. The total (negative) effect of aid on growth rate of GDP was smaller, but still near unity. On the other hand, in the savings equation, aid was not significant and negative but the total effect of aid on savings was noticeably positive. "How can foreign aid supplement domestic savings, which are low, and still retard economic growth?...The answer may be that foreign aid has been financing projects and programs whose overall benefits for the economy are negative...foreign aid will have no impact on the overall economic growth if the Government is not committed to a sound macroeconomic policy, expands unproductive expenses and accepts projects and programs imposed by donors which cannot be implemented for institutional and other constraints" (p. 103).

Dependency and world-system studies

The attempt to transform dependency into a 'theory of Latin American underdevelopment' and in some cases even into a theory of underdevelopment in the whole of the periphery was bound to succumb to the temptation to elaborate a corpus of formal and testable propositions which could by themselves explain the 'laws of motion of dependent capitalist underdevelopment'. Similarly, the attempt to construct a theory of this nature was bound to appear a seductive challenge for that part of the North American academic world which is ever anxious to consume unidimensional hypotheses referring to clearly established variables. While some are concerned to contribute to making the theory of underdevelopment consistent and operational, and therefore to seek to identify as clearly as possible a set of empirically testable hypotheses, with the aid of which they could construct a continuum running from 'dependence' to 'independence', others wish to demonstrate that this 'theory' has no 'scientific status,' as it has not constructed to date a model whose hypotheses pass the various tests of significance (Palma, 1978, p. 905).

Categorizing studies of the foreign capital (or aid) impact on economies of less developed countries by their theoretical perspective can generally be done quite easily. Studies from the dependency perspective and studies from the perspective of economic theory are found in different journals, by different authors, sometimes with little reference to the other. While researchers of dependency theory make reference to the 'other school' more often than did their counterpart economists, the focus was more on contradiction than on integration. And although their predictions regarding various relationships between domestic and foreign economic variables have many times been similar, they have not merged into a single stream of research.

One of the earliest studies of foreign capital in less developed countries from the dependency perspective was written by Paul Stevenson in 1972. His study attempted to "identify the impact of American direct investment in Latin America upon the economic growth rate of such countries...This study attempts to identify what variables seem to be preventing Latin America from reaching its economic growth goal" (p. 347). Stevenson used data from seven Latin American countries for the time period of 1961-67. His independent variables were direct investment from the United States, direct capital outflow to the US and foreign aid from the US (including military aid). The dependent variable was economic growth rate. His analysis included simple rank correlations, partial correlations and multiple correlations.

The results from multiple correlation found that from 1961-67 the amount of direct investment had increased, as variables had a strong negative relationship with economic growth in 1967 and a weak negative relationship in 1961. Stevenson concluded that the results indicated limited support for the 'neo-

Marxian' position (whereby investment and aid are detrimental to development). "American direct investment and American foreign aid were not positively associated with the economic growth rate of seven major Latin American countries, with the exception of Mexico, vis-a-vis direct investment" (p. 355).

The following year Tyler and Wogart (1973) also looked at the middle 1960's data in a cross-sectional analysis of 39 less developed countries. Their three measures of economic dependency were the ratio of foreign trade to GNP, the percentage of total exports represented by the two major commodities, and the ratio of exports going to the two major markets to total exports. As a dependent variable, Tyler and Wogart used the percentage of national income received by the poorest twenty percent, poorest sixty percent, and wealthiest five percent of the population. Their results supported the predictions of dependency theorists. Via bivariate regression, they found that dependency was negatively related to the percentage share of national income received by the poorest 20 percent and poorest 60 percent and that dependency was positively related to the percentage of income going to the richest five percent of the population. However, no control variables were introduced and there was a low percentage of variance explained, suggesting that factors other than economic dependence are important in determining income distribution (McGowan and Smith, p. 197).

In 1975, Kaufman, Chernotsky and Geller performed what they termed as a 'preliminary test of dependency theory', They "attempted to cull from the burgeoning theoretical literature a variety of disprovable, bivariate propositions which we operationalized and tested in the Latin American setting" (p. 303). They differentiated between two terms: trade dependency (which refers to the value of trade to the largest partner) and capital dependency (which refers to the current foreign public and private investment per capita). Utilizing four variables for trade dependency and four variables for capital dependency, their propositions covered the impact of dependency on land tenure structures, income distribution, balance of trade, levels of unionization, voting turnout, constitutional stability, and levels of militarism. Also they propositioned that, "countries with high levels of economic dependency are likely to have low rates of economic growth". Their operational measures of dependency tapped the extent of foreign involvement in Latin American economies, the degree to which a single metropolitan country dominates the flow of trade and the diversification or concentration of 'satellite' export structure. The time period used to test their proposition about growth rates was 1961-69. While inequality was positively related to economic dependency, contrary to their proposition, growth rates were positively associated with dependency indicators (from correlation matrices and multiple regression). Thus it may be that inequality was generated from capitalist growth, not dependency. From that and other results, they hypothesized that "if dependency produces inequality, it may well do so indirectly, through the stimulation of economic growth (and capital formation)" (p. 320). Overall, their results were mixed. They concluded that "the article shifts the burden of proof onto the shoulders of proponents of dependency theory" (p. 329).

According to Palma, the most sophisticated empirical study of this kind (as of 1978) was that of Christopher Chase-Dunn in December of 1975. The research employed was panel regression analysis which used 1950 and 1970 as its points in time (the number of cases ranged from 24 to 46). The dependent variables were per capita income, kilowatt hours of electricity consumed and the percent of males not employed in agriculture (all measures of economic development). The independent variables included international economic dependence per capita (measured as the profits made by foreign direct investment in the host country) and debt dependence per capita (external public debt). Domestic capital formation (savings), as a percent of GDP and specialization in mining were used as two control variables.

Chase-Dunn found that debt dependence did not facilitate economic development, and there was weak evidence that it retarded it. There was some support for the hypothesis that dependence caused unequal distribution of income. He concluded that "dependency theory must be taken seriously as an explanation for uneven development in the world economy...Foreign capital must be seen as a form of control as well as a flow of resources" (p. 735). The reasons for the results, he thought, were that dependent countries are not able to appropriate their own surplus capital for investment in balanced development; Transnational corporations operate for their own good, and use political and economic influence to keep labor costs and taxes low and to maintain the conditions for their continued profitable operation. "This growing awareness of the core-periphery contraction and the effects of dependence may be the beginning of a political process which eventually will modify the grossly uneven development of the world economy" (p. 736).

A 1976 study by Szymanski continued the investigation of dependency theory. Like Chase-Dunn, he only investigated growth in the manufacturing sector, ignoring overall economic growth. His cross-national study of Latin American countries covered the time period from 1960-72 and included five measures of aid and direct investment as indicators of dependency. Economic growth rates of Latin American countries were compared to those of some developed capitalist countries. Latin American rates were significantly lower. Bivariate rank-order correlation coefficients on US aid to Latin America were compared against a measure of overall structural aid dependency (accumulated US aid from 1945-74, divided by 1960 GDP). A positive but non-significant correlation was found between aid and economic growth for 19 countries. He concluded that neither dependency theory, nor liberal economic theory, could be completely supported. "One of the most interesting findings is that within the class of dependent countries the greater the dependence, the more rapid the rate of growth, even though the more dependent countries as a class are growing more slowly than the non-dependent countries" (p. 53). Szymanski did not investigate how profit repatriation affected growth, inequality or physical quality of life in Latin America and thus could not rule out that dependency may have had beneficial effects in spite of profit repatriation.

Szymanski characterized the results of his and previous studies of dependency as mixed: "Chase-Dunn showed more or less unconditional support of dependency theory; Stevenson (like Szymanski) correlates measures of dependence of Latin American countries with rates of growth (and finds) mixed evidence in favor of the dependency theory; three other studies (Griffin and Enos, Kaufman, et. al., Tyler and Wogart) concluded merely that dependency theory should not be rejected, since they were unable to find strong support for the thesis that dependency promotes clear and consistent economic development" (p. 54).

Rubinson (1977) contributed to the study by attempting to uncover intervening structural changes thought to produce a negative effect on economic growth in Dependence, Government Revenue and Economic Growth. The purpose was to specify the negative relationship between dependence and growth by studying the role of state strength. Two relationships were tested: the effect of dependence on state strength and the effect of state strength on economic growth. Dependency should have a negative effect on state strength and state strength should have a positive effect on economic growth, if the theory is correct. Dependence was measured as the value of imports and exports (high trade indicates high dependence), export partner concentration, external public debt, and value of debits in investment income (profits made by foreign direct investment in a country). State strength was measured by government revenues of a state as a proportion of GNP. Panel regression analysis was used, whereby the dependent variable was measured at 1955 and at 1970, and the independent variables were measured at 1955. The number of countries in the equations varied from 39 to 45. Among the findings was that two measures of dependence (export partner concentration and external public debt) negatively affected state strength, but the other two measures of dependence did not. The relationships were the same for rich countries as well. As for the effect of state strength on economic growth, it was positive and strong for poor countries; positive and weak for richer countries. They concluded that "most forms of economic dependence did have negative effects on economic growth and on state strength" (p. 24).

Conversely, Ray and Webster (1978) concluded that there was "strong evidence of a positive relationship between dependency and growth" after using the data of Kaufman et. al. (1977) with some modifications of the variables. Dependency was measured by trade commodity and export partner concentration, capital penetration, and trade composition. Economic growth was measured as the rate of growth of GNP. They also argued, though, that the strong relationship between dependency and economic growth does not imply the inapplicability of dependency theory when applied to Latin America.

52

After reviewing many of the previous studies of dependency theory, McGowan and Smith (1978) found that cumulative evidence provided thus far was not clear-cut enough to warrant policy recommendation. Their study introduced the variable of economic development potential in an effort to "expand our knowledge of the analytical usefulness of the concept of economic dependency itself and also the mechanisms through which dependency affects tropical African performance". The variable was operationalized as a state's known natural resources, capital, labor and technology. They distinguished between economic power dependency (resulting from the underdeveloped nature of the economy) and economic market dependency (resulting from reliance on the international market for goods, services, capital, and technology). Four variables for each type of dependency were correlated with 23 variables of economic performance. In general, their results did not support the contention that dependency stunts growth.

Their first test of dependency theory found that the percent of bilateral foreign aid from the major donor, and the three leading commodity exports as a percent of the total, were unrelated to a battery of 23 indicators of economic performance. However, there were many large and moderate positive correlations between economic performance and total trade value. Next they specified competing three-variable models relating economic dependency to economic performance and development potential. Thirty tropical African states were studied in the middle and late 1960's. Their analysis included bivariate analysis, multivariate analysis, and regression analysis. Little support was provided for the dependency based models.

In 1983, Kick and Conaty identified political and economic characteristics of Africa that were tied to post-colonial processes, including the penetration of Eastern and Western bloc states, and China. Two central contentions were presented: (1) Colonial Western hegemony was replaced by even more pervasive Western, Eastern, and Chinese competitive influences over control of African political economy; and (2) The external influence encompassed penetration effects that, depending on the source and time, alternately heighten or impede economic development in African countries. For 31 African countries they measured economic development as per capita income for the dependent variable. Independent variables included stock of Western foreign direct private investment (circa 1967, divided by 1965 GNP) which indicates foreign capital dependency; total net Western loans and grants (1960-66 divided by 1965 population) which indicates debt and grant dependence; grants and credits from the Eastern bloc and China; total foreign debt in 1967 (divided by 1965 GNP) to adjust for the effect on development of undifferentiated debt stock; annual military expenditures; and internal and extra-national warfare in Africa. Among their results was the finding that "Western investment and aid in the longer run have virtually no, or slightly negative, effects on per capita national wealth. Development depressing tendencies also appear to emerge for the longer-run impact of Chinese and Eastern bloc aid and for recent military expenditures. Economic development is encouraged in the short term by Eastern bloc assistance and in the longer run by military expenditures and undifferentiated debt stocks" (p. 283).

Bela Balassa (1986) reviewed a variety of interpretations of dependency theory and analyzed the key propositions that had been common to most writings on the subject. One of the 'principal tenants' of dependency theory identified by Balassa concerned the role of foreign capital. According to Balassa, dependency theory proposed that "foreign capital is increasingly directed to developing countries in search of high profits, which are then repatriated, counteracting the tendency of the declining rate of profit and permitting the payment of high wages to labour in the industrial countries" (p. 266). In contradiction to the proposition, Balassa found the share of the developing countries in the direct investment abroad of the US declined continuously during the post-war period. Latin America had a decline much in excess of the developing-country average. New investments in the developing countries also declined in relation to domestic investment in the US. Also, there was no evidence of super-profits being made in Latin America by US firms. From these findings, and investigation of other 'tenants' of the theory, Balassa concluded that "the propositions which have been put forward by dependency theorists do not stand up to scrutiny" (p. 270).

In a 1990 study, Lockwood used a sample of 91 third world countries to estimate the effects of aid on economic growth during 1970-78 and 1978-86. He found foreign aid to have short-term negative effects on economic growth during both time periods but long-term positive effects were significant for the later time period. From these results he concluded that "the dependency and world-system perspective must modify its theoretical explanations concerning the relationship between foreign capital flows and economic development to take into account the varied uses of different types of financial resources" (p. 11). He also noted that different phases of the expansion and contraction of the world economy might condition the effects of specific types of core-periphery interactions.

The recent experience of East Asian newly industrialized countries raised new questions about the development process and the roles of policy and foreign investment in the economic transactions between core and peripheral countries. Simeon Hein (1992) presented a model of the way in which national trade strategy, foreign investment, and economic growth might interact. First, he assumed that a policy of autonomous development in Latin America leads to an inward-oriented economy based on import substitution, and that outward-looking Asian countries seek economic interaction with the international economy which leads to growth. These two assumptions were used as a simplified hypothetical model to describe Latin American and East Asian development. The two policies of import substitution and export-led growth repel or attract foreign investment which he expected to affect economic growth by stimulating the domestic economy and creating new industries.

For the time period of 1970-73, Hein generated eight regression equations to test first the hypothesis that effects of policy, political instability and level of development explain levels of foreign investment, and second that policy, political instability, foreign investment and population growth explain per capita income growth. His results were "not consistent with predictions of the dependency theory and lent some support for the policy-development model" (p. 512). Outward-oriented economies were more dependent on foreign capital but grew faster than neutral or inward-oriented, less dependent countries. Foreign investment had no appreciable effect on growth; and political instability and population growth had a negative effect on foreign investment and economic growth. He concluded that medium-term economic growth has little to do with foreign investment and that states play a significant role in the development process. "If policy can be used to foster autonomous development, then the prospect that the state can deliberately encourage other types of development deserves further investigation...dependency theory appears underdeveloped specifically with respect to the role of the state" (p. 514).

Summary of previous studies

Overall, the results of studies testing the dependency theory have been mixed. Considering the inconsistencies in the variables used, time periods covered, countries included in the sample, types of analysis, etc., this is not surprising. Measures of dependency have included inflow of foreign direct investment, stock of foreign direct investment, profits earned from foreign investment, inflow of foreign aid (in only three studies), total value of loans and grants, outflow of capital, total value of trade, export partner concentration, export product concentration, external debt, etc. Dependent variables studied have included economic growth, income distribution, kilowatt hours of electricity consumed, and the percentage of males not employed in agriculture.

Time periods for the studies ranged from a few years to 20 years; samples ranged from a few countries in one geographical area to a large sample of less developed countries across all geographical areas. Methods of analysis have included correlational analysis, bivariate and multiple regression, panel regression analysis, etc. Finally, researchers have interpreted their results as: (1) mixed (Stevenson, Kick and Conaty); (2) neutral, such that dependency theory was not rejected (Tyler and Wogart, Kaufman et.al., Szymanski); (3) non-supportive (McGowan and Smith, Balassa, Hein); and (4) supportive (Chase-Dunn).

There appears to be some inconsistency as to where the burden of proof lies. Results have frequently been non-significant. Some researchers have interpreted non-significance as evidence against other theories and hence support for dependency theory. Others have interpreted non-significance as evidence against dependency theory. While interpretation of results does and should remain at the discretion of the researcher, the basis on which interpretations are drawn should be stated explicitly to control for individual bias as much as possible. This might also lead to a more consistent and methodical approach to studying development through the eyes of dependency.

Controversy remained the one constant among economists studying the relationship between foreign aid and economic growth. One generalization is the distinction between the orthodox position and its challengers. The orthodox position holds that all capital inflows are an addition to recipients' productive resources and thus increase economic growth. The Harrod-Domar and two-gap models were commonly used to demonstrate how capital inflows increased economic growth by easing domestic saving and/or foreign exchange gaps (e.g., Rosenstein-Rodan, 1961; Chenery and Strout, 1966). Griffin and Enos, Weisskoff, and others proposed instead that capital inflows lowered savings propensities and thus capital formation and economic growth. They made use of the same economic models but altered them to reflect a substitution effect between foreign aid and domestic savings. Papanek may be considered the moderate in this debate, holding the position that the data should answer the question. Other moderates include Stoneman, who distinguished between the effects from foreign capital flows and foreign capital stocks. Gupta also sought to refine the models to more properly specify the indirect effects of foreign capital through savings (Gupta and Islam, 1983, p. 22).

While there is some variation to the variables and approaches used, the model being tested has generally remained in the tradition of its Harrod-Domar and Chenery-Strout predecessors. All the studies of the past 20 years have used the same "basic explanatory variables" (foreign aid, domestic savings, and foreign investment). The importance of foreign exchange earnings from exports has also emerged in studies over the past ten years, which is consistent with the two-gap theory and was most likely brought into focus by the export-led growth of newly industrialized countries.

A more detailed summary of the major economic studies of aid effectiveness is given in Table 1. It is from this theoretical and empirical tradition that an 'initial' model for this study has been selected. The methodological approach, data sources, and estimation methods are explained in the following chapter.

3   A 'terminal' model is generated by replacing the expanded parameters into the initial model.

Generally speaking, the initial model represents an important relationship that has been taken from theoretical literature and empirical studies. The expansion equations model a possible contextual variation of the initial model. And the terminal model embodies the relationship and its contextual variations.

As implied earlier, the initial model expresses that economic growth may be explained by domestic savings, foreign investment, and trade (exports):

$$Y = a_0 + a_1 S + a_2 I + a_3 E \tag{5.1}$$

where Y denotes the real annual growth rate of GNP; S, annual domestic savings as a percent of GNP; I, annual foreign investment (foreign capital inflows) as a percent of GNP; and E, annual growth rate of exports. The parameters a_0, a_1, a_2, and a_3 of the initial equation in (5.1) are then expanded as functions of aid levels:

$$a_0 = c_{00} + c_{10} A \tag{5.2}$$

$$a_1 = c_{01} + c_{11} A \tag{5.3}$$

$$a_2 = c_{02} + c_{22} A \tag{5.4}$$

$$a_3 = c_{03} + c_{33} A \tag{5.5}$$

where A is annual official development assistance (aid) as a percent of GNP. The expansion equations are replaced back into the initial equation in (5.1) producing the following terminal equation:

$$Y = c_{00} + c_{10} A + c_{01} S + c_{11} S.A + c_{02} I + c_{22} I.A + c_{03} E + c_{33} E.A \tag{5.6}$$

A period between two variables indicates an interaction term.

Thus, the initial equation formulates the relationship between economic growth and savings, investment and exports. The expansion equations model the potential variation of the relationship between economic growth and its determinants in response to levels of economic aid. And the final (or terminal) equation captures both the initial model and its potential variation with aid.

The data and estimation of variables

The data for regressions are from the OECD's "Geographical Distribution of Financial Flows to Developing Countries: 1970-1990" (on diskette), and the World Bank's "World Tables: 1950-1988" (on magnetic tape). The number of less developed countries for the sample is 67. The time period is 1970-88.

GNP growth (Y)

The variable (Y) began as the World Bank's "constant 1980 price gross national product in local currency". It was then converted to US dollars using the World Bank's annual average exchange rate. To estimate the average real GNP growth rate over 19 years, the logged GNP of 1970 was subtracted from the logged GNP of 1988, and the difference was divided by 19.

Aid (A)

Previous studies of the aid-growth relationship have operationalized foreign aid in many ways. This may, in part, explain the differences in their findings. Previous studies have at times included military assistance; excluded all donors but the US; included non-concessionary transactions; etc.

Here, the variable (A) began as the OECD's "net disbursements of concessional assistance by DAC countries". According to OECD data consultant, Jean-Louis Grolleau, the term "concessional assistance" is synonymous with "official development assistance" Official development assistance, as the measure of aid, restricts the measure to only those foreign capital flows that contain concessionary elements and truly are donated for the expressed purpose of promoting the development of the recipient country. The OECD uses the terms aid, assistance, and official development assistance synonymously, meaning: "Grants or loans (1) undertaken by the official sectors, (2) with promotion of economic development or welfare as main objectives, (3) at concessional financial terms (if a loan, at least 25 percent grant element)" (OECD, 1992, p. A-99).

OECD data was expressed in US dollars at current average exchange rates. To compute aid as a percent of GNP, the OECD data was divided by the World Bank's "current price gross national product in local currency", which had been converted to US dollars using the World Bank's annual average exchange rate.

Domestic savings (S)

From the World Bank, "current prices gross domestic savings in local currency" was used and divided by the Bank's "current prices gross national product in local currency" to produce the variable (S), domestic savings as a percent of GNP.

Foreign capital inflows (investment) (I)

From the OECD, "net disbursements of concessional assistance by DAC countries" was subtracted from "total net disbursements of financial flows by DAC countries". The difference consists of (1) private flows, including direct investment, portfolio investment, and private export credit; and (2) official flows, including public export credit and long term capital which is not concessional. The data was expressed in current prices, US dollars. It was then divided by the World Bank's "current price gross national product in local currency", which had been converted to US dollars using the World Bank's annual average exchange rate. The result is (I), foreign inflow (or investment) as a percent of GNP.

Trade (exports) (E)

From the World Tables, "constant price exports, fob, in 1980 dollars" was used. The difference between each year's export value and the previous year's value was divided by the previous year's value, to determine the year's annual growth rate.

6 Results of Data Analysis

Regression specifications

The following notations will be used in the regression equations:

Y = GNP growth rate

A = official development assistance (aid) as a percent of GNP

S = domestic savings as a percent of GNP

I = foreign capital inflows (other than aid) as a percent of GNP

E = growth rate of exports

All variables are averages for the time period 1970-1988 and were calculated in constant 1980 US dollars. Aid flows include flows from members of the OECD's DAC (Development Assistance Committee) only. Members of the DAC include: Australia, Austria, Belgium, Canada, Denmark, Finland, France, Germany, Greece, Iceland, Ireland, Italy, Japan, Luxembourg, the Netherlands, New Zealand, Norway, Portugal, Spain, Sweden, Switzerland, Turkey, the United Kingdom and the United States.

The initial results presented refer to the equations below. A period between two variables indicates an interaction term.

$$Y = a_0 + a_2S + a_2I + a_3E + \varepsilon \tag{6.1.0}$$

i

$$a_0 = c_{00} + c_{10}A \tag{6.2.1}$$

$$a_1 = c_{01} + c_{11}A \tag{6.2.2}$$

$$a_2 = c_{02} + c_{22}A \tag{6.2.3}$$

$$a_3 = c_{03} + c_{33}A \tag{6.2.4}$$

$$Y = c_{00} + c_{10}A + a_1S + a_2I + a_3E + \varepsilon \tag{6.3.0}$$

$$Y = a_0 + c_{01}S + c_{11}S.A + c_{02}I + c_{22}I.A + c_{03}E + c_{33}E.A + \varepsilon \tag{6.4.0}$$

$$Y = c_{00} + c_{10}A + c_{01}S + c_{11}S.A + c_{02}I + c_{22}I.A + c_{03}E + c_{33}E.A. + \varepsilon \tag{6.5.0}$$

where ε is an error term and the usual assumptions apply; namely $E(\varepsilon_i)=0$, $E(\varepsilon_i^2)=\sigma^2$, and $E(\varepsilon_i\varepsilon_j)=0$.

Equation 6.1.0, the initial model, was taken from the traditional economic theory of growth. Equations 6.2.1 through 6.2.4 are expansion equations that allow the intercept and slopes of the initial model to be expanded for consideration of direct and indirect effects of Aid on the initial model. Equation 6.3.0 is the initial model with expansion of the intercept only, to allow consideration of the direct effect of Aid on the initial model; that is, is Aid related to economic growth directly? Equation 6.4.0, on the other hand, is the initial model with expansion of the slopes only, to allow consideration of only the indirect effect of Aid on the initial model; that is, how does aid modify the operation of other variables that are related to economic growth (for example, does aid enhance or lessen the relationship between savings, investment, or exports, and economic growth?). Finally, equation 6.5.0 is the terminal model that reflects the expansion of both intercept and slopes of the initial equation; it allows consideration of direct and indirect effects of aid simultaneously.

Data sample

From an original data set containing 97 less developed countries (as of 1970): 16 were removed due to missing data; four were removed because of negative average economic growth over 18 years (a reflection not of the ordinary processes of an economy but of extraordinary conditions); ten were removed that were outliers in every regression analysis, producing significant distortions in the parameter estimates; leavings a remaining sample of 67 less developed countries. Appendix A contains a list of countries in the sample and values for the dependent and independent variables.

Heteroscedasticity

Several tests for heteroscedasticity were performed on the residuals, on the basis of the Breusch-Pagan, Harvey, and Glejser tests, using the 'diagnos' command in SHAZAM. In doing so, the null hypothesis that there is no heteroscedasticity was tested. A rejection of the null hypothesis would indicate heteroscedasticity. In this case, the null hypothesis was not rejected, so there were no grounds for presuming heteroscedasticity.

Results

Table 2 provides a summary of the regression results.

Table 2
Regression Results for Total Sample

Equation 6.1.0
(FE) $Y = 0.032 + 0.010S + 0.014I + 0.041E$
         (0.682)   (0.258) (4.240)* $R^2 = .234$

(BS) $Y = 0.034 + 0.039E$
         (4.25)* $R^2 = .226$

Equation 6.3.0
(FE) $Y = 0.035 - 0.065A + 0.0002S + 0.021I + 0.039E$
         (-1.04)   (0.015)   (0.370) (3.99)* $R^2 = .248$

(BS) $Y = 0.034 + 0.039E$
         (4.25)* $R^2 = .226$

Equation 6.4.0
(FE) $Y = 0.029 + 0.044S - 1.07S.A + 0.016I - 0.061I.A + 0.028E + 0.489E.A$
         (2.12)* (-2.40)*   (0.262) (-0.030)   (1.16)   (0.614)

                                              $R^2 = .325$

(BS) $Y = 0.030 + 0.036S - 0.914S.A + 0.042E$
         (2.24)* (-2.71)*   (4.63)* $R^2 = .317$

Equation 6.5.0
(FE)
$Y = 0.025 + 0.074A + 0.056S - 1.24S.A + 0.018I - 0.035I.A + 0.041E + 0.125E.A$
      (0.713) (2.10)* (-2.44)*   (0.294)(-0.017)   (1.35)   (0.132)

                                              $R^2 = .331$
(BS) $Y = 0.030 + 0.036S - 0.914S.A + 0.042E$
         (2.24)* (-2.71)*   (4.63)* $R^2 = .317$

Note: 1. (FE) denotes forced entry of the full equation, whereby all variables in the
equation are entered in a single step.
2. (BS) denotes backward selection variable elimination with a probability of
F-to-enter of .05 and a removal value of .055.
3. t-values are in parentheses.
4. * significant at the 5.0% level or better.

Results from the initial model (Eq 6.1.0) indicate that of the variables savings, investment, and export growth, only export growth is significantly (and positively) related to economic growth. The direct relationship between aid and economic growth (Eq 6.3.0) is found to be negative, but not significant. Of the other variables in the equation, export growth alone is again positive and significant. From Equation 6.4.0, aid does, however, significantly and negatively modify the relationship between savings and growth. The direct relationship between savings and growth also become significant, while exports are significant only after backward selection. Finally, the terminal model (Eq 6.5.0) results in a significantly positive association between domestic savings with economic growth, and a significantly negative association between the interaction of savings and aid with economic growth. Again, the positive association of exports with growth becomes significant after backwards selection.

The results provide the basis for several interpretations of the relationships between economic growth and the variables aid, savings, investment and exports. First, the simple addition of aid as an independent variable (Eq 6.1.0), which is the typical approach to investigating the aid-growth relationship, finds the effect of aid to be not significant.

Second, it has been found that domestic savings is always positively associated with economic growth and the association is significant when the interaction of savings and aid has been accounted for. The interaction is always negative and always significant in its relationship with economic growth. This may be interpreted in at least two ways: (1) There is a selection effect, whereby aid flows were distributed to the lowest savers; or (2) Aid had a negative effect on savings, which has been suggested by earlier literature on economic theories and studies of growth. Previous studies have suggested that aid did not become a net addition to domestic savings. Instead, much of it went to increase consumption, having a negative effect on savings for two reasons: (a) Governments shifted money away from investment toward social programs or to lower taxes; and (b) Although the Chenery-Strout model indicated that the capital-output ratio is constant, it actually fell because donor governments insisted on monumental projects, rather than productivity investment (or because of tied aid which brought in donor goods at above market prices and left a need for spare parts or other goods from the donor) (Griffin, 1970; Griffin and Enos, 1970).

Third, export growth is positively associated with economic growth. But unlike savings, exports loses its significance when the indirect effect of aid is included (rather than gaining it, as in the case of savings). Also, while the interaction of exports and aid is positively associated with growth, the association is not significant.

Finally, it would appear from the results that while other foreign capital inflows are positively associated with economic growth, the association is not significant. It is noteworthy, however that the interaction of aid and investment is negative. Although the interaction is not significant in its relationship with growth, it does warrant some interpretation. Two logical interpretations are: (1) A selection effect, whereby aid flows went to countries with low levels of foreign investment but did not lead to significant levels of investment over time; or (2) Aid had a negative effect on foreign investment.

In sum, the terminal model found savings and export growth (after backward selection) to be significantly positive in their relationship with growth, and found the interaction of savings and aid to be significantly negative in its relationship with growth.

Sensitivity analysis

The question of how much confidence may be placed on the conclusions of cross-country regressions was addressed by Ross Levine and David Renelt in a 1992 American Economic Review article, "A Sensitivity Analysis of Cross-Country Growth Regressions". In their article a variant of Edward E. Leamer's (1983) extreme-bounds analysis (EBA) was used to test the robustness of coefficient estimates to alterations in the conditioning set of information. "Many candidate regressions have equal theoretical status, but the estimated coefficients on the variables of interest in these regressions may depend importantly on the conditioning set of information" (Levine and Renelt, p. 942).

The EBA here uses equations of the form: $Y = \beta_K K + \beta_A A + \beta_Z Z$ where Y is the dependent variable; L is a set of independent variables always included in the regression; A is the variable of interest; and Z is a subset of variables chosen from a pool of variables identified by past studies as potentially important explanatory variables. The EBA involves varying the subset of Z-variables included in the regression to find the widest range of coefficient estimates on the variable of interest, A, that standard hypothesis tests do not reject.

Levine and Renelt determined maximum and minimum coefficient values to examine if levels of significance and signs remain consistent for the variable of interest. If the coefficient remains significant and of the same sign at the extreme bounds, it is "robust". If not, it is "fragile". Here the variable of interest is aid and its interaction terms. Z-variables include a subset of variables in this example.

Results from the sensitivity analysis are shown below in Tables 3 through 6.

Table 3
Variable of Interest: Aid (A)

Sign of A Coefficient	Significant at 5% or better	t-value	Other Variables in the Equation
-		-1.569	S
-		-1.127	I
-		-1.271	E
-		-1.038	S, I, E
-		-1.597	S, I
-		-1.011	S, E
-		-1.253	I, E
+		.713	S, SA, I, IA, E, EA
-		- .237	S, SA
-		- .646	I, IA
-		- .918	E, EA

Table 4
Variable of Interest: Savings * Aid (SA)

Sign of SA Coefficient	Significant at 5% or better	t-value	Other Variables in the Equation
-	*	-2.147	S
-		-1.445	A, S
-	6.6	-1.871	S, I, IA
-		-1.476	A, S, I, IA
-	*	-2.740	S, E, EA
-	*	-2.696	A, S, E, EA
-	*	-2.404	S, I, IA, E, EA
-	*	-2.438	A, S, I, IA, E, EA

Table 5
Variable of Interest: Investment * Aid (IA)

Sign of IA Coefficient	Significant at 5% or better	t-value	Other Variables in the Equation
-		-1.038	I
-		-0.521	A, I
+		0.321	I, S, SA
+		0.417	A, I, S, SA
-		-0.973	I, E, EA
-		-0.924	A, I, E, EA
-		-0.030	I, S, SA, E, EA
-		-0.017	A, I, S, SA, E, EA

Table 6
Variable of Interest: Exports * Aid (EA)

Sign of EA Coefficient	Significant at 5% or better	t-value	Other Variables in the Equation
-		-0.876	E
+		0.141	A, E
+		0.817	E, S, SA
+		0.217	A, E, S, SA
-		-0.057	E, I, IA
+		0.467	A, E, I, IA
+		0.614	E, S, SA, I, IA
+		0.132	A, E, S, SA, I, IA

Results from the analysis yielded only fragile results, with the exception of the variable SA. The EBA on SA yields a nearly robust result. It can not be considered wholly robust because it is not significant at one of the extreme bounds. 'Nearly robust', however, seems a reasonable conclusion because EBA does result in a consistent coefficient sign, and significance in all but one case. Beyond these two findings, the tables help to clarify and reinforce the results of regressions shown in Table 2. First, Table 3 highlights the fact that aid is always associated negatively with growth, except in the terminal model. Thus, traditional approaches that examine aid as a single independent variable (where only a direct effect is examined) would appear to be incomplete. Here the negative effect between aid and growth is indirect, through the aid-savings relationship.

Second, as mentioned earlier, the manner in which savings and aid interact to negatively associate with growth is a nearly robust result. In other words, considerable confidence may be placed on this conclusion. Unfortunately, the analysis does not allow determination of whether the result is due to some type of selection effect (whereby aid is distributed to the lowest savers) or if there is a direct effect on saving rates from aid (as suggested by previous literature).

Third, although the result is not significant, aid seems to weaken the impact of investment on growth. Again, it can not be determined here as to whether aid is 'selected' for low investment sites, or if aid negatively affects foreign investment directly.

The lack of robustness found here is not surprising, as it is common to many studies of not only aid, but other explanatory variables of economic growth as well. "Many popular cross-country growth findings are sensitive to the conditioning information set. More fundamentally, they (the results) illustrate that it is very difficult to isolate a strong empirical relationship between any particular macroeconomic-policy indicator and long-run growth" (Levine and Renelt, p. 949).

Returning to the results in Table 2, the positive relationship between savings and exports with growth is well supported by theoretical and empirical literature. Results on the primary variable of interest, however, warrant further consideration. That is, further explanation of the significance of the savings-aid interaction and lack of significance for the direct aid-growth relationship is needed.

Further investigation

Negative correlation between savings and aid

The Harrod-Domar growth model (which expressed a relationship between savings, investment, and income) once provided the groundwork to predict that aid, as a supplement to investment, would raise domestic savings. In the 1970's, however, Griffin and Enos, as well as others, discovered through empirical work that the correlation between aid and savings was often negative, not positive. As mentioned above, two logical explanations of the significantly negative association between the savings-aid interaction and growth are that: (1) aid as a negative effect on savings; and (2) more aid goes to countries with low savings.

Donald Snyder (1990) referred to those who interpreted the negative savings-aid association as indication of a negative effect on savings from aid as "revisionists". Rahman (1968), Weisskopf (1972), Chenery and Eckstein (1970), and others supported this interpretation, proposing that aid-receiving countries increase government consumption and lower tax collection efforts (called "aid-switching"). Stewart (1971) and Papanek (1972) were among the critics of the revisionist hypothesis proposing instead that aid is distributed by need (savings levels) and/or that omitted variables are responsible for the negative correlation. Snyder (1990, p. 176) summarized the two camps as follows:

The Revisionist Case: Causation runs from aid to domestic savings; aid is exogenously determined according to the political preferences and self-interest of donors, with no regard for recipient need; aid is substituted for domestic savings.

The Revisionist Critics Case: No causation from aid to domestic savings; aid is given in response to recipient need, as measured by per capita income and (possibly) the savings ratio.

Snyder offered a model to analyze the specific effect of foreign aid (A) on savings (S), with explicit controls for the correlated effects of per capita income (Z). the model is as follows:

$$S = a_0 + a_1 Z + a_2 A \qquad\qquad (6.6.1)$$

$$A = b_0 + b_1 Z + b_2 S \qquad\qquad (6.6.2)$$

"Thus, domestic savings is a function of per capita income and foreign aid; and foreign aid is determined by need (donors are assumed to use low per capita income and/or low savings as indices of need)" (p. 176).

Snyder used ordinary least squares regression on fifty less developed countries for the period from 1960 to the early 1980's. In addition to the two equations shown above, he ran a bivariate regression with savings as the dependent variable and aid as the independent variable. His results may be summarized as follows:

1   From the bivariate regression, aid was negatively significant.

2   From equation 6.6.1, per capita income was positively significant and aid was negative and not significant.

3   From equation 6.6.2, per capita income was negatively significant and savings was negative and not significant.

Snyder concluded that while the negative savings-aid correlation that Griffin and Enos reported for the 1960's had persisted through the 1980's, "the highly significant coefficients for per capita income in both equations and the nonsignificance for the coefficients for (aid) and (savings)...supports the Stewart variant of the model as opposed to the revisionist position" (p. 177). Snyder would not, however, totally reject the revisionist position and conceded that "there may be a moderate tendency toward aid-switching by some countries" because the aid coefficient was consistently negative.

To help lend support to either the "revisionist camp" or its critics, Snyder's model will be tested here. The results are in Table 7 below.

Table 7
The Effect of Foreign Aid on Savings

	R^2
Equation 6.6.0	
S = -2.03 A	0.259
(-4.66)*	
Equation 6.6.1	
S = 0.038 Z - 1.64 A	0.316
(2.24)* (-2.97)*	
Equation 6.6.2	
A = -0.012 Z - 0.086 S	0.357
(-3.04)* (-2.97)*	

*Significant at 5% or better

Within the framework of Snyder's model, the results may be interpreted as follows:

1   The strong negative correlation between aid and savings is reconfirmed, for the 1970-88 time period.

2   Savings is a function of per capita income (positively) and aid (negatively), which according to Snyder would mean that aid does indeed lower savings.

3   Aid is a function of per capita income and savings (both negatively), which according to Snyder would mean that aid is given according to recipient need as indicated by a relatively low per capita income and low domestic savings.

It appears from the results above, that there is more than a "moderate tendency" toward aid switching. Snyder warned against the validity of other studies because often foreign capital inflow was used as a proxy for foreign aid, or net transfers received by governments plus official long-term borrowing was used, or sample sizes were small, etc. Those concerns do not apply here. The results strongly support both hypotheses as conclusively as is possible within the design of Snyder's model.

The design of Snyder's model, however, does not simultaneously address both hypotheses regarding the savings-aid relationship that are being debated. A different approach here analyzes both sides of the debate more directly. One hypothesis is that aid is primarily in response to recipient need, as indicated by low savings and per capita income levels (Equation 6.6.3). The other view is that aid is determined exogenously, and causes the savings rates of recipients to fall due to aid switching (as might foreign investment if it crowds-out domestic investment and hence savings) (Equation 6.6.4). Two stage least squares regression method (2SLS) is applied here to the following system of equations:

$$A = \alpha_0 + \alpha_1 S + \alpha_2 Z + \varepsilon_1 \qquad (6.6.3)$$

$$S = \Upsilon_0 + \Upsilon_1 A + \Upsilon_2 I + \varepsilon_2 \qquad (6.6.4)$$

where A is foreign aid as a percent of GNP; S is the domestic savings rate; Z is logged per capita income; and I is foreign investment. The results of the 2SLS method are as follows:

$$A = 0.200 + 0.173\ S - 0.029\ Z \qquad (6.6.3)$$
$$ (0.484)\quad (-1.07)$$

$$S = 0.284 - 4.42\ A + 0.794\ I \qquad (6.6.4)$$
$$ (-4.30)^*\quad (1.42)$$

$$n = 68$$

The results offer strong support for "revisionists" who argued negative causation from aid to savings, and only mixed support for "revisionists critics" who argued that negative associations were from higher aid allocation to lower savings. From equation 6.6.3, aid is given in response to recipient need, but not as measured by low savings rates, rather by low per capita income. In fact, there is a faint suggestion that among aid recipients with low per capita incomes, more aid goes to those with slightly better savings rates, rather than worse savings rates. Second, from equation 6.6.4, there is clear evidence that aid is affecting savings

75

rates negatively, presumable due to aid-switching. However, foreign investment enhances domestic savings, rather than crowding it out.

In summary (referring back to the terminal model (6.5.0)), the most appropriate interpretation of the significantly negative association between the savings-aid interaction and economic growth, is that (1) aid was given according to recipient need, as indicated by low per capita income; but (2) domestic savings rates have been significantly reduced in aid-receiving countries as a result of aid-switching.

Lack of significance for the direct aid-growth relationship

It is also important to investigate further the predominately negative but non-significant result for the direct aid-growth relationship. The result is not uncommon from previous studies. The simplest interpretation may be that aid flows are not large enough to have a significant effect on economic growth or are used in such a way that economic growth is unaffected (e.g., aid switching). However, it has also been suggested that aid flows are more or less effective at generating economic growth at different levels of economic development (Mosely, 1980). That is, the relationship between aid and growth should be considered within the framework of a country's level of development.

Recall that the initial model of economic growth (Equation 6.1.0) proposed that economic growth can be explained by domestic savings, foreign capital inflows, and exports. Only exports, however, were found to be significant, which leads to suspicion of the model itself. An alternative model to explain economic growth is the parabolic relation between per capita income and economic growth.

Casetti (1992) reviewed in detail the origins of this thesis and the empirical work that has supported it. The tendency for countries at an intermediate development level to grow faster can be supported by several perspectives. Rostow (1960) and Kahn (1976), for instance, might explain it as the onset of the transition from pre-modern stagnation to modern exponential growth. Gershenkron (1962) proposed that latecomers to development have an advantage over their predecessors such that the more delayed the industrial development of a country, the greater the 'spurt' of its industrialization because they have the benefit of learning from their predecessors. Others (Mattews, 1982; Olson, 1982) explain the parabolic phenomenon in terms of retardation of economic growth in mature economies.

As summarized by Casetti, three frames of reference are used to explain the parabolic relationship. The first is the rate of application of the existing stock of scientific and technological knowledge. The least-developed countries lack the capital, socio-economic structure, or labor power to apply much of the world's stock of knowledge and technology. The ability to use technology increases as they

76

develop. The developed countries, with a dwindling stock of unused technologies, become dependent upon creation of new knowledge and technology for growth (Kristensen, 1974; Casetti, 1992). This would produce a parabolic relationship between level of development and growth rate.

The second frame of reference involves the dynamics of capital formation and investments. Least-developed countries tend to have low savings rates and low capital-to-output ratios. Both begin to rise as a country develops, producing a phase of accelerated economic growth. Developed countries, on the other hand, tend to have a stronger preference for leisure and may divert savings toward consumption and welfare expenditures. Thus growth is slower at low and high ends of the scale.

The final frame of reference is the change in scale economies, whereby the mechanisms of increasing returns to scale and external economies that come with development, then decreasing returns to scale and external diseconomies, account for higher growth rates at intermediate development levels (Casetti, 1992, pp. 25-7).

The proposed income-growth relationship may be represented by the following equation:

$$Y = Z + Z^2$$

where Y is average annual GNP growth and Z is the logged per capita income level of the midpoint year for the time period in question. To investigate further the aid-growth relationship, the parabolic model will be used here as an initial model (6.7.0). The parameters a_0, a_1, and a_2 of the initial model will be expanded as functions of aid levels. The expansion equations [(6.8.1) through (6.8.3)] will be placed back into the initial model to produce a terminal model [equation (6.11.0)]. The terminal model captures both the initial model and its potential variation with aid, and thus allows determination of how the parabolic relationship between income and growth may be altered by economic aid. The regression equations are given below:

$$Y = a_0 + a_1Z + a_2Z^2 + \varepsilon \tag{6.7.0}$$

$$a_0 = c_{00} + c_{10}A \tag{6.8.1}$$

$$a_1 = c_{01} + c_{11}A \tag{6.8.2}$$

$$a_2 = c_{02} + c_{22A} \tag{6.8.3}$$

$$Y = c_{00} + c_{10}A + a_1A + a_2Z^2 + \varepsilon \tag{6.9.0}$$

$$Y = a_0 + c_{01}Z + c_{11}Z.A + c_{02}Z^2 + c_{22}Z^2.A + \varepsilon \qquad (6.10.0)$$

$$Y = c_{00} + c_{10}A + c_{01}Z + c_{11}Z.A + c_{02}Z^2 + c_{22}Z^2A + \varepsilon \qquad (6.11.0)$$

The sample and time period are the same as in the first regression analysis. Tests for heteroscedasticity were again performed on the basis of the Breusch-Pagan, Harvey, and Glejser tests, using the 'diagnos' command in SHAZAM. Again the null hypothesis of homoscedasticity was not rejected. The results are provided in Table 8.

Table 8
Regression Results

Equation 6.7.0

$Y = -0.116 + 0.047 Z - 0.004 Z^2$

         $(1.96)^*$ $(-2.00)^*$ $R^2 = 0.062$

Equation 6.9.0

$Y = -0.105 - 0.098 A + 0.046 Z - 0.004 Z^2$

         (-1.43) $(1.94) \otimes$ $(-2.05)^*$ $R^2 = 0.092$

Equation 6.10.0

$Y = -0.049 + 0.033 Z - 0.177 Z.A - 0.003 Z^2 + 0.026 Z^2.A$

         (1.32) $(-2.00)^*$ $(-1.60) \otimes$ $(1.85) \otimes$ $R^2 = 0.134$

(BS)

$Y = 0.063 - 0.215 Z.A - 0.0005 Z_2 + 0.032 Z^2.A$

         $(-2.55)^*$ $(-2.43)^*$ $(2.41)^*$ $R^2 = 0.110$

Equation 6.11.0

$Y = -0.040 - 0.523 A + 0.030 Z - 0.003 Z^2 + 0.011 Z^2.A$

         $(-1.80) \otimes$ (1.16) (-1.42) (1.51) $R^2 = 0.124$

(BS)

$Y = 0.063 - 0.658 A - 0.005 Z^2 + 0.014 Z^2.A$

         $(-2.48)^*$ $(-2.38)^*$ $(2.17)^*$ $R^2 = 0.105$

Note: 1. (BS) backward selection variable elimination with a probability of F-to-enter value of .05 and a removal value of .055.
2. t-values are in parentheses.
3. Significant at the 5% level or better.
4. $\otimes$ Significant at the 10% level or better.
5. The Z.A interaction term was removed from the terminal model as a result of multiple regression because the minimum tolerance level of .0001 was reached.

The results may be summarized as follows:

1   From the initial model (6.7.0), the parabolic relation between per capita income (Z) and economic growth (Y) is significant, indicating economic growth is positively associated with per capita income up to a point, after which time growth slows as per capita income continues to rise.

2   The direct relationship between aid (A) and growth, when per capita income has been controlled for (6.9.0) is negative and strong, but not significant.

3   The interaction terms [from equation (6.10.0)] indicate that aid has a significant indirect relationship with growth, through its modification of the initial model (6.7.0); and

4   From the terminal model (6.11.0) and from backward selection, direct and indirect effects of aid on growth, and the parabolic relationship between income and growth are significant.

In summary, a parabolic relationship with a maximum between income level and growth does occur [equation (6.7)]. And while the coefficient for aid as an independent variable is negative, the interaction of logged per capita income squared and aid is positively associated with growth. This implies that the parabolic income-growth relationship differs (or shifts) across the context of aid flows (that is, the aid-growth relationship differs across levels of income).

Thus, further investigation of the nonsignificance found initially for the aid-growth relationship yields important results. The parabolic relationship between income level and growth appears to be a normal pattern, at least for the less developed countries in this study. Aid flows, however, alter the pattern of growth through levels of income. A particularly intriguing interpretation comes to mind; until per capita income reaches a certain threshold level, the aid-growth relationship is significantly negative (Z.A from 6.10.0). From investigation of the negative savings-aid correlation and previous literature, this may be due to significant aid switching and inappropriate aid utilization within the poorest recipient countries and/or because during pre-takeoff stages, preparation for take-off may actually lessen economic growth for some time.

After the threshold is reached, however, aid becomes a measurably positive contributor to growth as income rises (although growth rates tend to slow as income rises) (Z^2.A from 6.10.0 and 6.11.0).

The regression results also allow estimation of the threshold level of per capita income where the aid-growth relationship moves from negative to positive.

The derivative (dY/dA) was calculated from the terminal model (6.11.0) to evaluate the change in growth associated with a unit increment in aid.

$$dY/dA = -0.523 + 0.011 \, Z^2 \qquad\qquad (6.11.0)$$

$$Z^* = 6.895 \qquad\qquad (\text{logged})$$

$$y^* = \$987.64 \qquad\qquad (\text{unlogged})$$

where $Z = \ln(y)$, y is GNP per capita, and Z^*, y^* are threshold values.

For values of Z smaller than 6.895, aid has a negative effect on growth, while for values of Z greater than this threshold, the effect of aid on the rate of growth is positive. Z is the logarithm of per capita income, which means that in terms of these results, aid has a perverse effect on development for per capita income smaller than $987 and positive effects on it at levels of per capita income greater than $987.

Thus, the relationship between aid and economic growth is negative where per capita income is lower than $987, and positive for countries with a high per capita income. This may be illustrated graphically as well. From the terminal model (6.11) two graphs were generated.

In Figure 1, two parabolas represent the income-growth relationship with and without aid. Growth levels are higher for countries *without* aid, when income levels are below the threshold level. Growth levels are higher *with* aid when income levels are above threshold level. Figure 2 shows how dramatically different the aid-growth relationship appears on different sides of the threshold. Specifically, Figure 2 shows the aid-growth relationship at income levels of respectively $500, $1,000, and $1,500 per capita.

A summary of all results from this study and the conclusions that may be drawn from them are presented in the following chapter.

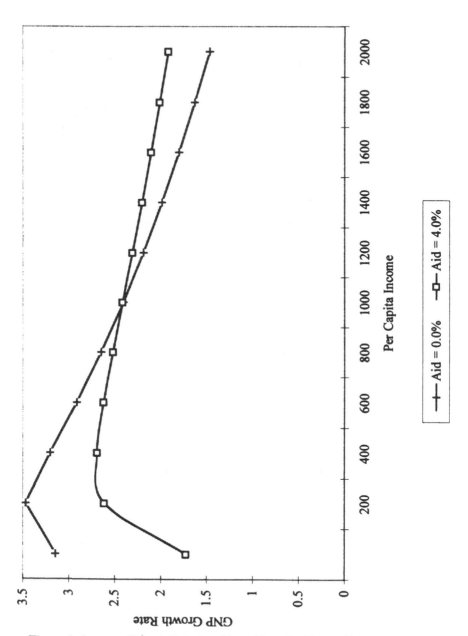

Figure 1: Income-Growth Relationship, with and without aid

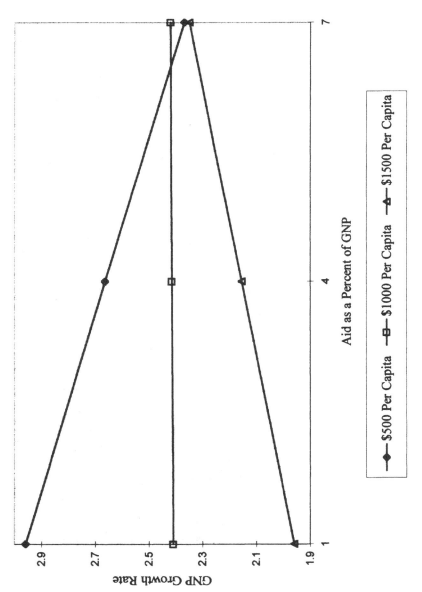

Figure 2: Aid-Growth Relationship, by income level

7 Discussion of the Study

Introduction

Despite more than forty years and nearly a trillion dollars of foreign aid, surprisingly little is known about the impact of aid on economic growth in recipient countries. Whether reviewing theoretical literature, or previous empirical research, the aid-growth relationship remains controversial.

No single theory or model adequately explains the role of foreign and domestic capital in the growth of less developed economies. However, three 'standard explanatory variables' are found in many studies. These are foreign aid, domestic savings, and foreign investment. More recently, export growth has been added to the list of standard determinants of economic growth in less developed countries. The origins of these variables can be traced to the Harrod-Domar and Chenery-Strout models.

Studies that have focused specifically on the role of aid in economic growth most frequently test the aid-growth relationship by treating aid as an independent variable along with savings, foreign investment, and exports and employing ordinary least squares regression. The results have been mixed, with as many non-significant results as significant results. This may be due to differences in samples, time periods, variable measures, etc., or may be due to inadequacy of the model being tested.

A basic premise of this study is that aid is not adequately tested by the 'standard' model which investigates it only as a separate independent variable, and ignores its relationship with other determinants of economic growth. The expansion methodology allows more effective investigation of the direct and indirect relationships between aid and economic growth by taking the initial model and expanding its parameters as functions of aid levels to generate a terminal model that includes both direct and indirect aid-growth relationships. In other

84

words, the terminal model generated by expansion methodology investigates not only the standard direct relationships, but also investigates the indirect aid-growth relationship, vis-a-vis aid interaction with other determinants of growth.

This study was conducted on a sample of 67 less developed countries, with data averaged over a 19 year period (1970-1988).

Summary of results

The results from the initial model were consistent with previous studies: the direct aid-growth relationship was not significant, nor were most of the other direct relationships in the model. Expansion of the initial model, however, uncovered an indirect aid-growth relationship via its interaction with domestic savings, which was significant and negative.

A sensitivity analysis of the result found it to be quite strong (nearly robust), and reflective of either a selection effect (whereby low savings rates led to high aid level, but not to economic growth) and/or a causal aid-savings relationship (whereby aid caused savings rates to fall due to aid-switching).

To determine the most appropriate explanation, two-stage least squares regression analysis was applied to a system of equations modeling the aid-savings relationship. The results found low per capita income, rather than low savings rates, lead to high aid levels. Evidence that aid was affecting savings rates negatively (presumably due to aid-switching) was also found.

Thus by expanding the standard initial model to consider aid interactions with other independent variables, aid was found to not be significantly associated with economic growth directly; however, aid was found to have substituted for domestic savings within aid-receiving countries.

Further investigation of the aid-growth relationship was conducted by replacing the first model of economic growth with an alternative model exploring economic growth rates by level of development. This model, which originated from both theoretical and empirical literature, proposed that countries at an intermediate development level grow faster than countries below or above that level. Previous studies have found the parabolic relationship between income level and growth to be a typical pattern. Expansion methodology allowed investigation of whether or not aid flows altered this pattern of growth by level of income for the sample and time period covered by this study.

The results confirmed the parabolic income-growth relationship whereby economic growth is positively associated with per capita income up to a point, after which growth slows as income continues to rise. It was also found that the pattern of growth was significantly altered by aid flow. In sum, prior to the peak of the income-growth parabola (below some threshold level of income), the aid-growth relationship was negative; past the peak of the parabola (above threshold level) the aid-growth relationship was positive. The threshold level of income was found to be approximately $1,000.

Thus an additional explanation for the initially significant aid-growth result of this and other studies may be proposed. The aid-growth relationship varies across level of development. Therefore, investigations of a linear aid-growth relationship for all income levels find a non-significant result because, in essence, negative and positive relationship at different income levels "cancel" each other out.

Conclusions

The accumulation of results contained in this study suggest the following conclusions:

1   Aid has been given in response to recipient need, proxied by per capita income level.

2   In countries with a per capita income of less than approximately $1,000 (roughly 55% of the sample), aid has been substituted (or switched) for domestic savings, coinciding with low economic growth.

3   In countries with per capita income above $1000, aid has been positively associated with growth, either because switching behavior by recipient governments was reduced as income rose (allowing aid to act as a supplement to domestic capital formation rather than as a substitute), or because the effectiveness of other determinants of growth increased with level of development.

Clearly the role of domestic government policies which affect aid-switching is in need of further investigation. The nature of government policies toward aid within recipient countries and how those policies differ across countries (particularly across per capita income levels) is a question that must be better answered to arrive at conclusions about aid effectiveness, and that cannot be answered using traditional methodologies and techniques found in economic literature alone.

8   Additional Comments

The current context for development assistance

Tisch and Wallace (1994) note that development aid has lost its novelty. The problems identified in the 1950's and 1960's have only grown more difficult, more frustrating, and have lost their glamour. Much of the challenge today is administrative and bureaucratic.

The context in which foreign assistance programs operate has changed significantly in recent years. The most notable change is the end of the Cold War which had served as the ideological paradigm of many aid programs. The end of the Cold War also greatly increased the number of nation-states seeking assistance, and aid flows shifted somewhat toward these states at the expense of others. Simultaneously, bilateral aid budgets in many countries have been cut due to domestic political and social pressures. Only the bilateral aid budget of Japan has significantly increased over the past 20 years. This in turn heightens the role of multilateral institutions for the next century. Also, moral questions continue to plague aid-granting institutions regarding the true beneficiaries of their activities.

But while the context has changed dramatically, the mechanisms continue, based in large part on the "Western model of development assistance", whereby donors provide funding on a project basis; donors manage projects with expatriate professionals; and donors design, implement, and evaluate, all within a short time horizon to 'prime the pump' of economic growth (Tisch and Wallace). Based on a functional perspective, it postulates that "if economic growth is stimulated by ODA, the inequities and injustices supported by undeveloped economies will be reduced" (p. 121). The core causes of underdevelopment and poverty are left largely unaddressed. If the model is changing at all, it is through the increasing role of NGOs (non-government organizations) as they become more involved in policy and issue consultation.

Fortunately, they note, the model has provided enough success (that it can assist governments committed to growth-oriented economic policies) to encourage future efforts. And the need for development assistance remains: "Great differences exist in living standards between rich and poor countries, and the global community can not afford to lose its members to hunger" (p. 135).

The future of the regime

Robert Wood (1996) outlines the aid regime's evolution, its current status and its future. Like Tisch and Wallace's contention that the Western model of assistance remains intact following the end of the Cold War, the same is true for Wood's over-arching aid regime. While Cold War politics were a central rationale for aid programs, there were always others and they persist (from self-interested export promotion to religious and secular humanitarianism).

It seems paradoxical that as the number of donors and recipients increase, with ever more complex and ambiguous motives and objectives, the regime grows stronger and tighter around the choices of recipient governments. The end of the Cold War leaves recipient governments with fewer choices about conditions to be met for external assistance. More specifically,

> we are likely to see the extension and consolidation of a number of currently tentative regime norms linking aid allocation and concessionality more closely to economic performance and sustainable development. In a context of increased competition for aid resources, graduation practices within the regime will likely be tightened, shifting countries sooner from more to less concessional aid and then to market mechanisms (Wood, p. 35).

Unfortunately, the study conducted here, and others, have found that aid has performed least well where it is most needed (in the poorest countries). Thus the evolving norms of the regime, it seems, will become increasingly inappropriate for the neediest countries. R.H. Cassen (1988) holds that poor aid coordination and lack of an enabling environment of institutions, labor, and information flows are the problem preventing aid effectiveness in the least developed countries.

> It is these countries that most need assistance to iron out disabling fluctuations of the international economy and *where prevailing adjustment strategies are least promising*...While others have graduated out of aid receiving and more will follow, the poorest will stay in those ranks for the foreseeable future. We should think about their long-term development and the role of aid in that perspective (italics added) (p. 180-81).

Shifts within the aid regime following the Cold War appear as follows: bilateral and multilateral donors increasingly target non-project funds to promote free-market reforms, reduced roles for government, and multi-party elections within recipient states based in part on their economic performance, with an eye on graduation to non-concessional financing; recipient states face increasing competition for aid and a narrowing range of choices about the conditions that must be met to receive aid; and the poorest recipient states, where aid has been least successful (as confirmed by this study and others), and where structural adjustment programs may be particularly inappropriate, are least able to compete for aid and are simultaneously experiencing a deterioration in their economic and social conditions (as well as high population growth rates). The regime is poised to exacerbate the national inequities and human suffering it should be working to alleviate.

Bibliography

Abou-Settit, M.F. (1986), 'Foreign Capital and Economic Performance: The Case of Egypt', Dissertation, The University of Texas at Dallas.

Akef, M.A. (1988), 'The Economics of Development Assistance: The Egyptian Case', Dissertation, Colorado State University.

Alschuler, L. (1976), 'Satellitization and Stagnation in Latin America', *International Studies Quarterly*, Volume 20, pages 39-82.

Amin, G. (1995), *Egypt's Economic Predicament*, Leiden, Brill.

Amin, S. (1974), *Accumulation on a World Scale: A Critique of the Theory of Underdevelopment*, New York, Monthly Review Press.

_____ (1975), 'Towards a New Structural Crisis of the Capitalist System' in C. Widstrand, ed., *Multinational firms in Africa*, Institute for Economic Development and Planning, pages 3-56.

_____ (1990), *Maldevelopment: Anatomy of a Global Failure*, Tokyo, United Nations University Press.

Areskong, K. (1969), *External Borrowing: Its Role in Economic Development*, New York, Praeger.

_____ (1973), 'Foreign Capital Utilization and Economic Policies in Developing Countries', *Review of Economics and Statistics*, Volume 55, pages 182-89.

Baer, W. (1969), 'The Economics of Prebisch and ECLA', in C. Nisbet, ed., *Latin America: Problems in Economic Development*, New York, Free Press.

Balassa, B. (1986), 'Dependency and Trade Orientation', *World Economy*, Volume 9, Number 3, pages 259-73.

Bandow, D. and I. Vasquez (1993), 'The Dismal Legacy and False Promise of Multilateral Aid', in D. Bandow and I. Vasquez, eds., *Perpetuating Poverty*, Washington, CATO Institute.

Baran, P. (1957), *The Political Economy of Growth*, New York, Monthly Review Press.

Baran, P. and P.M. Sweezy (1966), *Monopoly Capital*, New York, Monthly Review Press.

Bauer, P.T. (1966), 'Foreign Aid: An Investment for Progress?', Woodward Lecture given at Yale University, reprinted in B. Wart and P.T. Bauer, 'Two Views on Aid to Developing Countries', Occasional Paper 9, Institute of Economic Affairs.

_____ (1981), *Equality, The Third World, and Economic Delusion*, Cambridge, Harvard University Press.

_____ (1982), 'Foreign Aid: What Is At Stake?', *The Public Interest*, Summer.

_____ (1984), *Reality and Rhetoric*, London, Weidenfeld and Nicolson.

Bauer, P. and Yamey (1978), in W.S. Thompson, ed., *The Third World: Premises of US Policy*, San Francisco, Institute for Contemporary Studies.

Bergsten, C.F., R.O. Keohane and J.S. Nye Jr. (1975), 'International Economics, International Politics: A Framework for Analysis', in C.F. Bergsten and L.B. Krause, eds., *World Politics and International Economics*, Washington, The Brookings Institute.

Bergsten, C.F., T. Horst and T.H. Moran (1978), *American Multinationals and American Interest*, Washington, The Brookings Institute.

Blaug, M. (1990), *John Maynard Keynes: Life, Ideas, Legacy*, London, The MacMillan Press Ltd.

Bornschier, Volker and Ballmer-Cao (1978), *Multinational Corporations in the World Economy and National Development: an Empirical Study of Income per Capita Growth 1960-1975*, Bulletin of the Sociological Institute of the University of Zurich, Number 32, Zurich, Sociological Institute of the University of Zurich.

Bornschier, V., C. Chase-Dunn and R. Rubinson (1978), 'Cross-National Evidence of the Effects of Foreign Investment and Aid on Economic Growth and Inequality', *American Journal of Sociology*, Volume 84, pages 651-83.

Bornschier, V. and T.H. Ballmer-Cao (1979), 'Income Inequality: A Cross-National Study', *American Sociological Review*, Volume 44, pages 487-506.

Braungart, R. and M. Braungart (1979), 'Axes of World Structure and Conflict, Multinational Corporations and Nation-States', *Humboldt Journal of Social Relations*, Volume 6, pages 4-45.

_____ (1980), 'Multinational Corporate Expansion and Nation-State Development: A Global Perspective', in L. Kriesberg, ed., *Research in Social Movements, Conflicts and Change*, Volume 3, Greenwich, JAI Press, pages 169-186.

_____ (1981), 'Nation-State Development, Multinational Corporate Growth and Citizenship: A Theoretical Comparison', *Humboldt Journal of Social Relations*, Volume 8, Number 2, pages 48-78.

Brown, W. (1953), *American Foreign Assistance*, Washington, Brookings Institute.

Browne, S. (1990), *Foreign Aid In Practice*, London, Pinter Publishers Limited.

Cardoso, F.H. (1972), 'Dependency and Development In Latin America', *New Left Review*, Volume 74, pages 83-95.

_____ (1973), 'Associated-dependent Development: Theoretical and Practical Implications', in Alfred Stephan, ed., *Authoritarian Brazil*, New Haven, Yale University Press, pages 142-76.

Cardoso, F.H. and E. Faletto (1978), as quoted by G. Palma, 'Dependency: A Formal Theory of Underdevelopment or a Methodology for the Analysis of Concrete Situation Underdevelopment', *World Development*, Volume 6, Number 7/8, pages 881-924.

Carty, R. and V. Smith (1991), *Perpetuating Poverty: The Political Economy of Canadian Foreign Aid*, Toronto, Between the Lines.

Casetti, E. (1972), 'Generating Models by the Expansion Method: Applications to Geographical Research', *Geographical Analysis*, Volume 4, pages 81-91.

_____ (1982), 'Mathematical Modeling and the Expansion Method', in R.B. Mandel, ed., *Statistics for Geographers and Social Scientists*, New Delhi, Concept Publishing.

_____ (1986), 'The Dual Expansion Method: An Application for Evaluating the Effects of Population Growth on Development', *IEEE Transactions on Systems, Man and Cybernetics*, Volume 16, Number 1, pages 29-39.

_____ (1990), 'The Investigation of Parameter Drift by Expanded Regressions: Generalities and a 'Family Planning' Example', *Environment and Planning*, Volume 23, pages 1045-1061.

Casetti, E. and J.P. Jones III (1987), 'Spatial Applications of the Expansion Method Paradigm', in C. Durfournaud and D. Dudycha, eds., *Quantitative Analyses in Geography*, Department of Geography Publications Series Number 26, University of Waterloo.

_____ (1992), 'An Introduction to the Expansion Method and To Its Applications', in J.P. Jones III and E. Casetti, eds., *Applications of the Expansion Method*, New York, Routledge.

Casetti, E. and K. Tanaka (1992), 'The Spatial Dynamics of Japanese Manufacturing Productivity: An Empirical Analysis By Expanded Verdoorn Equations', *Journal of the RSAI*, Volume 71, Number 1, pages 1-13.

Chase-Dunn, C.K. (1975), 'The Effects of International Economic Dependence on Development and Inequality: A Cross-National Study', *American Sociological Review*, Volume 40, pages 720-38.

Chenery, H.S. (1979), *Structural Change and Development Policy*, New York, Oxford University Press.

_____ (1986), *Industrialization and Growth: A Comparative Study*, New York, Oxford University Press.

Chenery, H.S. and M. Bruno (1962), 'Development Alternatives in an Open Economy: The Case of Israel', *Economic Journal*, March.

Chenery, H.S. and A.M. Strout (1966), 'Foreign Assistance and Economic Development', *American Economic Review*, Volume 56, pages 679-733.

Chenery, H.S. and I. Adelman (1966), 'Foreign Aid and Economic Development: The Case of Greece', *Review of Economics and Statistics*, February.

Chenery, H.S. and P. Eckstein (1970), Development Alternatives for Latin America', *Journal of Political Economy*, July/August.

Chenery, H.S. and M. Syrquin (1975), *Patterns of Development, 1950-70*, London, Oxford University Press.

Chilcote, R.H. (1974), 'Dependency: A Critical Synthesis of the Literature', *Latin American Perspective*, Volume 1, Number 1, pages 4-29.

_____ (1984), *Theories of Development and Underdevelopment*, Boulder, Westview Press.

Cho, G. (1995), *Trade, Aid, and Global Interdependence*, London, Routledge.

Choi, K. (1983), *Theories of Comparative Economic Growth*, Ames, The Iowa State University Press.

Chowdhury, A. and C. Kirkpatrick (1994), *Development Policy and Planning*, London, Routledge.

Coleman, D. and F. Nixson (1986), *Economics of Change in Less Developed Countries*, Second Edition, Oxford, Philip Allan Publishers.

Dacy, D.C. (1975), 'Foreign Aid, Government Consumption, Savings and Growth in Less Developed Countries', *Economic Journal*, Volume 85, pages 548-61.

De Silva, L. (1984), *Development Aid: A Guide to Facts and Issues*, Geneva, UN-NGLS and Third World Forum.

Deane, P. (1978), *The Evolution of Economic Ideas*, Cambridge, Cambridge University Press.

Domar, E.D. (1946), 'Capital Expansion, Rate of Growth, and Employment', *Econometrica*, Volume 14, pages 137-47.

_____ (1989), *Capitalism, Socialism, and Serfdom: Essays*, Cambridge, Cambridge University Press.

Dos Santos, T. (1970), 'The Structure of Dependence', *American Economic Review*, Volume 60, pages 231-36.

_____ (1973), 'The Crisis of Development Theory and the Problem of Dependence in Latin America', in H. Bernstein, ed., *Underdevelopment and Development*, Harmondsworth, Penguin Books, pages 57-80.

Dowling, J.M. and U. Hiemenz (1983), 'Aid, Savings and Growth in the Asian Region', *The Developing Economies*, Volume 21, pages 3-13.

Elkan, W. (1995), *An Introduction to Development Economics*, Hempstead, Prentice Hall/Harvester Wheatsheaf.

Enos, J.L. and K.B. Griffin (1975), 'An Example of the Attribution Problem: Rejoinder to Over', *Economic Development and Cultural Change*, Volume 24, pages 757-59.

Essuman, J.W. (1987), 'External Financing and Economic Growth in Sub-Saharan Africa', Dissertation, University of Wisconsin-Madison.

Evans, P. (1979), *Dependent Development: The Alliance of Multinational, State, and Local Capital in Brazil*, Princeton, Princeton University Press.

Farmer, B.R. (1996), 'Toward A Comparative Study Of Dependency and Economic Development: Measurement and Analysis', Dissertation, Texas Tech University.

Floto, E. (1975), *Partners in Dependency: The Case of Private Foreign Capital in the Andean Group*, Cambridge, University of Cambridge Working Papers Number 23.

Foster-Carter, A. (1974), 'Neo-Marxist Approaches to Development and Underdevelopment', in E. De Kadt and G. William, eds., *Sociology and Development*, London, Tavistock.

Frank, A.G. (1966), 'The Development of Underdevelopment', *Monthly Review*, Volume 18, pages 17-31.

_____ (1969), *Latin America: Underdevelopment or Revolution*, New York, Monthly Review Press.

_____ (1974), 'Dependence is Dead, Long Live Dependence on the Class Struggle: A Reply', *Latin American Perspective*, Volume 1, Number 1, pages 87-106.

_____ (1975), *On Capitalist Underdevelopment*, Bombary, Oxford University Press.

_____ (1979), *Dependent Accumulation and Underdevelopment*, New York, Monthly Review Press.

Friedman, T.L. (1997), 'Globalization and US Foreign Policy', speech at the Aspen Institute, Aspen, CO, © 1997 Purdue Research Foundation.

Frondizi, S. (1947), *La Integracion Mundial, Ultima Etapa Del Capitalismo*, Buenos Aires, Praxis.

_____ (1957), *La Realidad Argentina: Ensayo De Interpretacion Sociologica*, Buenos Aires, Praxis.

Furtado, C. (1964), *Development and Underdevelopment*, Berkeley, University of California Press.

_____ (1970), *Economic Development of Latin America*, London, Cambridge University Press.

_____ (1973), *Underdevelopment and Dependence: The Fundamental Connection*, Cambridge, University of Cambridge Press.

Gerschenkron, A. (1962), *Economic Backwardness in Historical Perspective*, New York, F.A. Praeger.

Gilpin, R. (1975), *US Power and the Multinational Corporation*, New York, Basic Books.

Goulet, D. and M. Hudson (1971), *The Myth of Aid: The Hidden Agenda of the Development Reports*, prepared by the Center for Development and Social Change, International Documentation on the Contemporary Church, New York, Orbis Books.

Griffin, K. (1970), *Underdevelopment in Spanish America*, London, George Allen and Unwin.

_____ (1970), 'Foreign Capital, Domestic Savings, and Economic Development', *Bulletin of the Oxford University Institute of Economics and Statistics*, Volume 32, pages 99-112.

Griffin, K. and J.L. Enos (1970), 'Foreign Assistance: Objectives and Consequences', *Economic Development and Cultural Change*, Volume 18, pages 313-27.

Gupta, K.L. and M.A. Islam (1983), *Foreign Capital, Savings and Growth*, Dordrecht, D. Reidel.

Harrod, R.F. (1939), *Towards A Dynamic Economics*, London, MacMillan and Co., Ltd.

Hayden, B. (1987), 'Policy and Economics and Foreign Aid', *Economic Analysis and Policy*, Volume 17, Number 1, pages 1-15.

Hayter, T. (1971), *Aid As Imperialism*, Hardmondsworth, Middlesex, Penguin Books.

_____ (1981), *The Creation of World Poverty*, London, Pluto Press.

Hayter T. and C. Watson (1985), *Aid: Rhetoric and Reality*, London, Pluto Press.

Hein, S. (1992), 'Trade Strategy and the Dependency Hypothesis: A Comparison of Policy, Foreign Investment, and Economic Growth in Latin America and East Asia', *Economic Development and Cultural Change*, Volume 40, Number 3, pages 495-521.

Hirschman, A.O. (1958), *The Strategy of Economic Development*, Yale University Press.

Hook, S.W. (1995), *National Interest and Foreign Aid*, Boulder, Lynne Rienner.

_____ (1996), 'Foreign Aid and the Illogic of Collective Action', in S.W. Hook, ed., *Foreign Aid Toward the Millennium*, Boulder, Lynne Rienner.

Hope, K.R., Sr. (1996), *Development in the Third World: From Policy Failure to Policy Reform*, Armonk, M.E. Sharpe.

Hoselitz, B.F. (1960), *Sociological Aspects in Economic Growth*, Glencoe, Free Press.

Islam, M.N. (1982), 'Domestic Growth Factors, Foreign Economic Influences, and Third World Development: A Multivariate Test of Theories of Development', Dissertation, Syracuse University.

Jalee, P. (1968), *The Pillage of the Third World*, New York, McGraw-Hill.

Jepma, C.J. (1992), *LDC Financial Requirements*, Aldershot, Avebury.

Kaufman, R.H., H. Chernotsky and D. Geller (1975), 'A Preliminary Test of the Theory of Dependency', *Comparative Politics*, Volume 7, pages 303-330.

Kellman, M. (1971), 'Foreign Assistance: Objectives and Consequences', *Economic Development and Cultural Change*, Volume 20, pages 144-47.

Kennedy, C. and A.P. Thirlwall (1971), 'Foreign Capital, Domestic Savings, and Economic Development: Comment', *Bulletin of the Oxford Institute of Economics and Statistics*, Volume 32, pages 135-38.

Keohane, R.O. and V.D. Oooms (1975), 'The Multinational Firm and International Regulation', in C.F. Bergsten and L.B. Krause, eds., *World Politics and International Economics*, Washington, The Brookings Institute.

Kick, E. and J. Conaty (1983), 'African Economic Development: The Effects of East, West, and Chinese Penetration', in A. Bergesen, ed., *Crises in the World System*, Beverly Hills, Sage.

Kimaru, C.M. (1996), *International Charity for Self Interest: US Foreign Policy Toward Tropical Africa in the 1980's*, New York, Nova Science.

Kindleberger, C.P. (1975), 'The MNC in a World of Militant Development Countries', in G. Ball, ed., *Global Companies*, Englewood Cliffs, Prentice-Hall, pages 70-84.

Krauss, M. (1983), *Development Without Aid*, New York, McGraw-Hill.

Kuznets, S. (1963), 'Notes on the Take-Off', in W.W. Rostow, ed., *The Economics of Take-Off into Sustained Growth*, London, Macmillan.

Lall, S. (1975), 'Is Dependence a Useful Concept in Analyzing Underdevelopment?', *World Development*, Volume 3, pages 799-910.

Landau, D. (1990), 'Public Choice and Economic Aid', *Economic Development and Cultural Change*, pages 559-75.

Lappe, F.M., J. Collins and D. Kinley (1980), *Aid as Obstacle: Twenty Questions About Our Foreign Aid and the Hungry*, San Francisco, Institute for Food and Development Policy.

Lavy, V. and E. Sheffer (1991), *Foreign Aid and Economic Development in the Middle East*, New York, Praeger.

Lensink, R. and P. Van Bergeijk (1991), 'Official Finance Requirements in the 1990s', *World Development*, Volume 19, Number 5, pages 497-510.

Linear, M. (1985), *Zapping the Third World: The Disaster of Development Aid*, London, Pluto Press.

Lockwood, W.G. (1990), 'Foreign Aid and Economic Growth in Developing Countries', Dissertation, The University of Arizona.

Magdoff, H. (1969), *The Age of Imperialism*, New York, Van Nostrand Reinhold Company.

_____ (1976), 'The MNC and Development: A Contradiction?', in D.E. Apter and L.W. Goodman, eds., *The MNC and Social Change*, New York, Praeger.

McClelland, D.G. (1966), 'The Impulse of Modernization', in M. Weiner, ed., *Modernization: The Dynamics of Growth*, New York, Basic Books.

McDaniel, T. (1976), 'Class in Latin America', *Berkeley Journal of Sociology*, Volume 21, pages 27-50.

McGowan, P. and D. Smith (1978), 'Economic Dependency in Black Africa: a Causal Analysis of Competing Theories', *International Organization*, Volume 32, Number 1, pages 179-235.

McNeill, D. (1981), *The Contradictions of Foreign Aid*, London, Croom Helm.

Mikesell, R.F. (1983), *The Economics of Foreign Aid and Self-Sustaining Development*, Boulder, Westview Press.

Mosley, P. (1980), 'Aid, Savings, and Growth Revisited', *Bulletin of Economics and Statistics*, Volume 42, pages 79-97.

_____ (1987), *Overseas Aid: Its Defense and Reform*, Brighton, Harvester Press.

Mosley, P., J. Hudson and S. Horrell (1987), 'Aid, the Public Sector and the Market in Less Developed Countries', *Economic Journal*, Volume 97, pages 616-41.

_____ (1992), 'Aid Effectiveness and Policy', in G. Bird, ed., *International Aspects of Economic Development*, Guildford, Surrey University Press.

Myrdal, G. (1957), *Economic Theory and Underdeveloped Regions*, London, G. Duckworth.

_____ (1968), *Asian Drama: An Inquiry Into the Poverty of Nations*, New York, Pantheon.

_____ (1970), *The Challenge of World Poverty*, New York, Pantheon.

Newark, J.W. (1995), 'Foreign Aid in the 1990s: The New Realities', in M. Dorraj, ed., *The Changing Political Economy of the Third World*, Boulder, Lynne Reinner.

Nurske, R. (1953), *Problem of Capital Formation in Underdeveloped Countries*, Oxford, Blackwell.

O'Brien, P.J. (1975), 'A Critique of Latin American Theories of Dependency', in I. Oxall, T. Barnett and D. Booth, eds., *Beyond the Sociology of Development, Economy and Society in Latin America and Africa*, London, Routledge and Kegan Paul.

OECD (1981), *DAC 1981 Review*, Paris, OECD.

_____ (1985), *Twenty-five Years of Development Cooperation: A Review*, Paris, OECD.

_____ (1992), *Development Co-operation: Efforts and Policies of the Members of the Development Assistance Committee*, Paris, OECD.

Olaniyan, R.O. (1996), *Foreign Aid, Self-Reliance, and Economic Development in West Africa*, Westport, Praeger.

Over, A.M. (1975), 'An Example of the Simultaneous Equations Problem: a Note on "Foreign Assistance: Objectives and Consequences"', *Economic Development and Cultural Change*, Volume 24, pages 751-56.

Palma, G. (1978), 'Dependency: A Formal theory of Underdevelopment or a Methodology for the analysis of Concrete situations of Underdevelopment?', *World Development*, Volume 6, pages 881-924.

Papanek, G.F. (1972), 'The Effect of Aid and Other Resource Transfers on Savings and Growth in Less Developed Countries', *Economic Journal*, Volume 82, pages 934-50.

_____ (1973), 'Aid, Foreign Private Investment, Savings, and Growth in Less Developed Countries', *Journal of Political Economy*, Volume 81, pages 120-30.

_____ (1983), 'Aid, Growth and Equity in southern Asia', in J. Parkinson, ed., *Poverty and Aid: Essays in Honor of Just Faaland*, Oxford, Basil Blackwell.

Payaslian, S. (1996), *US Foreign Economic and Military Aid*, Lanham, University Press of America.

Poon, J. (1992), 'Manufactured Exports and Economic Growth', Dissertation, The Ohio State University.

_____ (1994), 'Export Growth, Economic Growth and Development Levels: an Empirical Analysis', *Geographical Analysis*, Volume 26, Number 1, pages 53-8.

Prebisch, R. (1950), *The Economic Development of Latin America and Its Principal Problems*, New York, United Nations.

_____ (1971), *Change and Development*, New York, United Nations.

Rahman, A. (1968), 'Foreign Capital and Domestic Savings', *Review of Economics and Statistics*, February.

Rana, P. and J.M. Dowling (1988), 'The Impact of Foreign Capital on Growth: Evidences from Asian Developing Countries', *The Developing Economies*, Volume 26, pages 3-11.

Riddell, R.C. (1987), *Foreign Aid Reconsidered*, Baltimore, The Johns Hopkins University Press.

Rosenstein-Rodan, P.N. (1943), 'Problems of Industrialization of Eastern and South-Eastern Europe', *Economic Journal*, Volume 53, pages 202-11.

_____ (1961), 'International Aid for Underdeveloped Countries', *Review of Economics and Statistics*, Volume 43, pages 107-38.

_____ (1964), *Capital Formation and Economic Development*, Cambridge, The M.I.T. Press.

Rostow, W.W. (1956), 'The Take-Off Into Self-Sustained Growth', *Economic Journal*, Volume 66, pages 25-48.

_____ (1971), *The Stages of Economic Growth: A Non-Communist Manifesto*, Second Edition, London, Cambridge University Press.

Rubinson, R. (1977), 'Dependence, Government Revenue, and Economic Growth: 1955-70', *Studies in Comparative International Development*, Volume 12, pages 3-28.

Ruttan, V. (1989), 'Why Foreign Economic Assistance?', *Economic Development and Cultural Change*, pages 411-23.

Seers, D. (1963), 'The Limitations of the Special Case', *Bulletin of the Oxford Institute of Economics and Statistics*, Volume 25, pages 77-98.

Smith, A. (1978), 'The Case of Dependency Theory', in W.S. Thompson, ed., *The Third World: Premises of US Policy*, San Francisco, Institute for Contemporary Studies.

Smith, B. H. (1990), *More Than Altruism: The Politics of Private Foreign Aid*, Princeton, Princeton University Press.

Stepan, A. (1978), *The State and Society: Peru in Comparative Perspectives*, Princeton, Princeton University Press.

Stevenson, P. (1972), 'External Economic Variables Influencing the Economic Growth Rate of Seven Major Latin American Nations', *Canadian Review of Sociology and Anthropology*, Volume 9, pages 347-56.

Stewart, C. (1975), 'Foreign Capital, Domestic Savings, and Economic Development: Comment', *Bulletin of the Oxford Institute of Economics and Statistics*, Volume 32, pages 138-49.

Stoneman, C. (1975), 'Foreign Capital and Economic Growth', *World Development*, Volume 3, pages 11-26.

Streeten, P. (1980), 'From Growth to Basic Needs', in P. Streeten, ed., *Development Perspectives*, London, MacMillan Press.

Sunkel, O. (1969), 'National Development Policy and External Dependence in Latin America', *Journal of Development Studies*, Volume 6, Number 1, pages 23-48.

_____ (1974), 'External Economic Relations and the Process of Development: Suggestions for an Analytic Framework', in R.B. Williamson, W.P. Glade Jr. and K.M. Schmitt, eds., *Latin American-US Economic Interrelations*, Washington, American Enterprise Institute for Public Policy Research.

Sweezy, P.M. (1972), 'Sociological Transformations in Developing Countries', *Intermountain Economic Review*, Volume 3, Number 1, pages 1-6.

_____ (1972a), 'A Reply to Charles T. Nisbet', *Intermountain Economic Review*, Volume 3, Number 1, pages 73-6.

_____ (1978), 'Corporations, the State and Imperialism', *Monthly Review*, Volume 30, Number 6, pages 1-10.

Szymanski, A. (1976), 'Dependence, Exploitation, and Economic Growth', *Journal of Political and Military Sociology*, Volume 4, pages 53-65.

_____ (1981), *The Logic of Imperialism*, New York, Praeger.

Thirlwall, A.P. (1989), *Growth and Development*, London, MacMillan Education Limited.

Tisch, S.J. and M.B. Wallace (1994), *Dilemmas of Development Assistance: The What, Why, and Who of Foreign Aid*, Boulder, Westview Press.

Todaro, M.P. (1981), *Economic Development in The Third World*, Second Edition, New York, Longman.

United Nations (1960), *International Economic Assistance to Underdeveloped Countries*, UN Document E/3395, New York, United Nations.

_____ (1965), *Report on the World Social Situation*, New York, United Nations.

_____ (1974), *Multinational Corporations in World Development*, New York, Praeger.

Wall, D. (1973), *The Charity of Nations: The Political Economy of Foreign Aid*, New York, Basic Books.

Wallerstein, I. (1974a), *The Modern World System I: Capitalist Agriculture and the Origins of the European World Economy in the Sixteenth Century*, New York, Academic Press.

_____ (1974b), 'The Rise and Future Demise of the World Capitalist System: Concepts for Comparative Analysis', *Comparative Studies in Society and History*, Volume 16, pages 387-415.

_____ (1980), *The Modern World System II: Mercantilism and the Consolidation of the European World Economy 1600-1750*, New York, Academic Press.

Warren, B. (1980), *Imperialism: Pioneer of Capitalism*, New York, New Left Books.

Weisskopf, T. (1972), 'The Impact of Foreign Capital Inflow on Domestic Savings in Underdeveloped Countries', *Journal of International Economics*, Volume 2, pages 25-42.

Wilson, R. (1995), *Economic Development in the Middle East*, London, Routledge.

Wood, R. (1980), 'Foreign Aid and the Capitalist State in Underdeveloped Countries', *Politics and Society*, Volume 10, pages 1-34.

_____ (1986), *From Marshall Plan to Debt Crisis*, Berkeley, University of California Press.

_____ (1996), 'Rethinking Economic Aid', in S.W. Hook, ed., *Foreign Aid Toward the Millennium*, Boulder, Lynne Rienner.

World Bank (1984), *World Debt Tables, 1988-89*, Washington, World Bank.

Zimmerman, C.C. (1970), 'The Sociology of Change in the Underdeveloped Lands', in C.C. Zimmerman and R.E. Du Wors, eds., *Sociology of Underdevelopment*, Vancouver, C. Clark Publishing Co.

For Product Safety Concerns and Information please contact our EU representative GPSR@taylorandfrancis.com Taylor & Francis Verlag GmbH, Kaufingerstraße 24, 80331 München, Germany

Printed and bound by CPI Group (UK) Ltd, Croydon, CR0 4YY

08/05/2025

01864463-0001